As a parent of three Gen Z kids myself, I  how Jason's book touches on a broad arra͏ this generation. It's easy to get stuck focusi͏ng on one or another, but this book is a practical guide to taking a step back, looking at the full landscape of Gen Z concerns, and evaluating when and where parenting adjustments would be helpful. More importantly, *Parenting Gen Z* will leave you encouraged—not overwhelmed!

NATASHA CRAIN, speaker, podcaster, and author of *Faithfully Different*

Parenting Gen Z is an absolute must-read! You might be overwhelmed, confused, and worried as a parent, but that's understandable, and Jason Jimenez won't shame you at all. He brilliantly explains how changes in our culture have influenced many children's beliefs, then describes how you can influence their thinking and behavior. (He's not afraid to tackle any topic!) His writing is engaging, his comparisons make learning easy, and his illustrations help the truth come alive, making it easier to successfully implement the many practical suggestions. You'll want to keep the book handy, since there is so much hope in these pages. This book needed to be written, and Jason is definitely qualified.

KATHY KOCH, PhD, founder of Celebrate Kids, Inc., and author of *Screens and Teens, 8 Great Smarts, Start with the Heart,* and *Resilient Kids*

Many of us know that raising kids today is more challenging than ever before, but a lot of parents can't explain why that is. Why does parenting in the twenty-first century seem so difficult? Jason Jimenez has done us parents a huge service: His book helps us *know* our Gen Z kids so that we can truly *help* them. He provides insights into what kids today think and value, the cultural forces that shape their hearts and minds, and the challenges they face. And it's only after we understand Gen Z that we'll be able to meet them where they're at and effectively guide them toward Christian maturity. Jason also provides a wealth of tools and action steps, making this book a truly practical guide for all parents.

BRETT KUNKLE, president of MAVEN and coauthor of *A Practical Guide to Culture: Helping the Next Generation Navigate Today's World*

Parenting is hard! When our culture is moving as fast as it is today, and with the unprecedented challenges Gen Z is facing, parents need all the help we can get! No one parents perfectly, but that doesn't mean you can't be faithful and intentional as you raise your kids to follow Jesus. I'm excited that Jason Jimenez has written *Parenting Gen Z* to equip and encourage parents as they seek to pass on their faith to the next generation. This timely book will help prepare you for the challenges and opportunities along the way.

JONATHAN MORROW, director of cultural engagement and student discipleship at Impact 360 Institute, author of *Welcome to College*, and creator of the course 5 Things Every Teenager Needs to Build a Lasting Faith

In *Parenting Gen Z*, our buddy Jason Jimenez has created a masterful, reader-friendly guide for parents raising kids in a crazy world. We love Jason's bold stance on many hot topics and the care he shows as he teaches parents how to exercise their authority with confidence. Jason offers fresh ideas that we, as dads, are sure to implement in raising our own kids.

DAVID AND JASON BENHAM, entrepreneurs and coauthors of *Whatever the Cost* and *Living Among Lions*

Parents today face lots of pressure and chaos in this ever-changing world, and *Parenting Gen Z* does a wonderful job in bringing peace and order to this chaos. Jason Jimenez provides a well-defined understanding of the issues at hand, and he does so in a way that feels like a conversation. His clear and doable action steps caused me to reflect and embrace more intentional practices with my kids. While the parenting journey is daunting, Jason's book is full of hope and encouragement for parents who want God's best for their children. As a pastor and a dad, I am excited to share this book with the parents I know!

PATRICK McCRORY, generations pastor at Carmel Baptist Church

With just the right balance of eye-opening statistics, practical advice, and real-world perspective, *Parenting Gen Z* is a must-read for any parent, teacher, or youth leader who wants to lead this generation well. Jason Jimenez pulls back the curtain on the struggles, fears, and doubts our kids are facing—often unbeknownst to us—while offering parents plenty of hope and helpful tips to move forward in love. Highly recommended!

BRITTANY ANN, founder of EquippingGodlyWomen.com and author of *Fall in Love with God's Word* and *Follow God's Will*

Every generation exhibits the beauty and brokenness of humanity. Jason Jimenez offers an eye-opening look at the tendencies of Gen Z, providing practical advice on how to engage and influence them with the truth about who they are—and who God is.

SARAH STONESTREET, cohost of the *Strong Women* podcast and mom to four Gen Zers

Parenting
GEN

Guiding
Your
Child

through
a Hostile
Culture

JASON JIMENEZ

FOCUS
ON THE FAMILY®

A Focus on the Family resource
published by Tyndale House Publishers

To my wife, who exemplifies God's grace and has helped shape me into the father I am to our four children.

To my dearest children: Tyler, your character is admirable. Amy, your passion for truth is contagious. Jackson, your empathy is laudable. Hailey, your love for life is remarkable.

I love you all!

Contents

Introduction

Gen Z Parents Are Overwhelmed

PARENTS TODAY are in panic mode.

"We don't know what else to do," one desperate mother told me. She and her husband had been trying for years to get their teenage son some help for his depression. "Nothing seems to work." Their son remains despondent and shut off from the rest of the world.

Another parent, a man in his mid-forties, said he felt like a failure and blamed himself for his two grown sons' loss of faith. With eyes filled with tears and a crack in his voice, this father pleaded for God's help as he and I prayed for his hope to renew and that his sons would one day return to faith in Christ.

Along with increasing cases of depression and abandoned faith among their children, a growing number of parents are facing the challenges that come with learning that a son or daughter is either gay or gender confused. Almost without fail, parents will come up after I speak somewhere and ask for advice on dealing with a child who identifies as gay or transgender. Some want to know how to balance unconditional love without compromising their beliefs; others want to know how they missed the signs. I can still hear the sobs of a woman who broke down as she shared how her daughter had disowned her family after marrying an older woman right out of high school. "I just want my baby girl back," the mother pleaded.

Perhaps you can relate to these parents. Perhaps not.

— — —

As a father of four Gen Zers, and as a pastor who has worked with parents and students since the late 1990s, I doubt I am overstating it when I say that Gen Z is probably the most challenging generation to raise in American history. And if you're raising a member of Generation Z—children born between 1997 and 2012—you are likely dealing with your own challenges. Indeed, my wife and I have endured feelings of pressure, stress, and anxiety over our kids. For example, would it surprise you to hear that the members of this generation are becoming the leading consumers of sexually explicit material online?[1] It's no wonder parents are concerned.

When I first started working with millennials (the generation preceding Gen Z), I encountered enormous challenges. Many in this age group came from broken families and had very little knowledge about the Bible. Every week I counseled parents whose kids were taking drugs and/or having premarital sex.

Fast forward to today: Parents of Gen Zers are dealing with far more complicated and disturbing concerns. The spread of secularism is more evident among Gen Z. The influence of social media and technology on our kids is more profound. Racial and political divides have led to ever more violence. And, of course, we can't ignore the mass shootings that seem to occur almost weekly in America's schools. These are matters of grave concern, and I will address each of them.

To do this, I've divided the book into four parts. In part 1, "Getting to Know Gen Z," we'll explore the eight core characteristics of Gen Z, the categories of parents raising Gen Z, and three common parenting flaws related to this generation. In part 2, "Concerns Facing Gen Z," we'll confront together the real issues facing Gen Z and discuss approaches for engaging our kids on controversial topics. In part 3, "How to 'Keep It 100' While Raising Gen Z," we'll look at God's design for the family, what parental discipline looks like, and some adjustments we can make to help create more time with our kids. In part 4, "Forging a Pathway for Gen Z," we'll learn biblical strategies to increase our impact at home, review five ways to help discover and nurture the future God has for our children, and consider some special encouragement for single parents.

Let me be clear: I didn't write this book because I've figured everything out as a parent. Not even close. I'm not some sort of parenting master. But I will say that this book is based on honesty, fervent prayer, lessons learned through my mistakes, and the successes that we've shared together as a family.

As a pastor, youth pastor, and apologetics speaker, I want to help parents leverage their authority and gifts in the home, and I hope to enable as many young people as possible to find their true identity and satisfaction in Christ.

In *Parenting Gen Z*, my goal is to help you become the parent God calls you to be. This book is designed to equip you with the tools you need not only to combat the many influences threatening Gen Z but also to earn your child's respect as you speak truth into his or her life. In straightforward and practical ways, I will explain how to parent Gen Z with wit, discernment, and plenty of biblically based wisdom. To help me with this task, I'll lean heavily on several godly and respected voices in my life—people I look up to and admire for the way they've raised their own kids. Finally, I'll draw on the countless hours I've spent with Gen Zers—both my own children and others—learning what makes them tick so that I might give you an accurate picture of their generation.

You need to know that I'm not going to sugarcoat who Gen Zers are or attempt to downplay the significant challenges you and I are facing as their parents. We'll discuss a lot of the worrisome aspects of this generation. We'll also address some of the common flaws in parenting them. Just as important, we'll touch on the good that exists within Gen Z and the amazing opportunity that you, Mom and Dad, have been given to raise these kids. And at the end of nearly every chapter, you'll find a "Parenting Practice" section with extra tips to incorporate into your family life.

Parenting Gen Z can feel overwhelming at times, but God doesn't want you to worry. He has given you everything you need (2 Peter 1:3-9) to get the job done as a parent. (Yes, even if you are a single parent!) The Bible makes it clear that God will keep you from stumbling (Jude 1:24). As you remain faithful to your calling as a Christian parent, you will reap the rewards of your labor (Ephesians 6:8).

I only ask that you give this book a chance. My aim is to help strengthen your parenting skills. Let's work together to build a lasting legacy that will encourage Generation Z to love God and live for His purposes.

So what are we waiting for? Let's embark on this journey together.

Jason Jimenez

PART ONE

GETTING TO KNOW
GEN Z

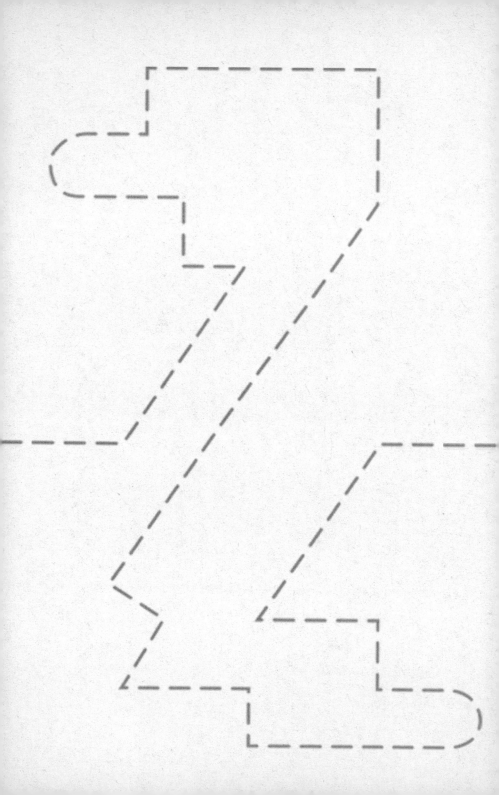

1

WHO IS GEN Z?

YOU MAY OR MAY NOT have heard of the band Twenty One Pilots, but chances are that your Gen Z kid has.

Multiple writers have described the Ohio duo as "the band of Generation Z," largely because their lyrics address the doubts, angst, and confusion that this generation faces. In their hit song "Stressed Out," Twenty One Pilots front man and chief songwriter Tyler Joseph introduces an enigmatic character he calls Blurryface.

You might be scratching your head right now, wondering what on earth is a Blurryface. I'll do my best to explain.

To fans of the band, Blurryface represents the insecurities and emotions that many Gen Zers attempt to conceal from others—with varying degrees of success. A closer look at Gen Zers revealed to me that they are experiencing symptoms of stress and depression on a greater scale than previous generations. And because of increased suicide rates among their peers, Gen Zers are burying more friends than any other generation. Beginning with the bloodshed at Columbine High School and the terrorist attacks of 9/11, Gen Zers have grown up in a world of violence, mass shootings, cyberterrorism, and media hysteria, creating yet another label for Gen Z: "The School Shooting Generation."[1]

Add in the emergence of a global pandemic that threw Gen Z into a tailspin—schools closed, graduations canceled, and job opportunities evaporated—and it's no wonder that Gen Z is weary and struggling to keep it together. As one sixteen-year-old told me, "I feel like all I do is worry about what's to come."

This is where Blurryface comes in. Near the end of the first verse, all his Gen Z angst comes to the forefront: "I was told when I get older, all my fears would shrink. But now I'm insecure, and I care what people think. *My name's Blurryface and I care what you think*" (emphasis added).[2]

As the song continues, Blurryface laments the loss of a carefree youth—when he dreamed of rocket ships and outer space, when his mom sang him to sleep at night. But now he's preoccupied with student loans and the pressure of making money. In many ways, Blurryface truly embodies Gen Z—transitioning from a world of youthful make-believe to a place where people are stressed out by the pressures and insecurities of life.

I care what you think.

While folks of any age can become addicted to social media, Gen Zers are more likely than most to obsess over what others think of them. Frantically checking online to see if people liked or commented on their posts is a way to reassure themselves that they are seen and affirmed. Many times, it's not about needing people to agree with their points of view as much as it is seeking validation for who they are—for their very existence.

I care what you think.

EIGHT TRAITS

For much of recent history, millennials (those born between 1981 and 1996) have gotten most of the attention, casting a shadow on Gen Z. But here's the thing: Gen Z represents nearly as many people as the millennial generation. We're talking about a difference of only a few million. There are roughly seventy-two million millennials, while Gen Z is more than sixty-eight million strong.[3] There are even some estimates that say Gen Z outnumbers millennials.[4] Regardless of which generation represents the greater numbers, a significant question remains: Which generation will have the greatest impact? Many signs point to Gen Z.

Some Gen Zers are at the age when they're beginning to impact the world economy, global politics, educational policies, and business in general. They may be getting married, starting families, and making decisions about the role of religion in their lives. To better understand Gen Z, we should first recognize that it's virtually impossible to identify every single trait common to this generation. That's just part of the challenge when trying to decipher the true meaning behind a character like Blurryface.

In the rest of this chapter, I will do my best to shed some light on Gen Z by laying out eight core traits of this generation:

1. Divergent Identity
2. Significant Creativity
3. Religious Uncertainty
4. Sexual Fluidity
5. Ethnic Diversity
6. Progressive Mentality
7. Language Sensitivity
8. Emotional Instability

Your child may not manifest each and every trait. That's to be expected. These eight core traits paint a collective picture of Gen Z, not of particular individuals. As we dig deeper into these character traits, we'll better understand and relate to our kids' generation. This new level of understanding can help us as we pursue stronger and more intimate connections with our children and as we seek to raise them according to God's principles.

First Trait: Divergent Identity

Gen Z is not just a bunch of smartphone addicts. They are a divergent generation. In Veronica Roth's popular young adult book *Divergent*, the main character, Tris Prior, in many ways represents Gen Z.

Divergent takes place in a dystopian future where humans are divided into five factions based on individual defining traits. When Tris enters adulthood, she undergoes an aptitude test designed to determine her distinctive trait. Her test results, however, are inconclusive. Tris realizes her identity is not reflective of any single faction. Her inconclusive results make her "divergent"—in other words, like much of Gen Z today.

A taste of Gen Z's divergence was on full display in 2019 when the *New York Times* surveyed hundreds of Gen Zers for a multimedia presentation titled "900 Voices from Gen Z, America's Most Diverse Generation." The finished product includes quotes from young people across the social and geographical spectrum. As I read through each one, several quotes stood out. Take this one from Andrew, born in 1997: "I am a gay Chinese-American cis man raised in Xian, China, and Boone, N.C., with the ability to immerse in white Southern culture as well as the communist society of China." Will, born in 1999, declares, "I'm both queer and Black, which is a weird combination for ever feeling like I truly fit in anywhere." Mary, from Wyoming, defines herself as a gender-nonconforming "gay multiracial girl."[5]

How does one define a generation when that same generation is self-admittedly in a constant state of flux? The idea that one's identity and expression of that identity can change over time is referred to as *fluidity*. A 2019 report titled "Into Z Future" from the Innovation Group explored the habits, influence, and expectations of Gen Z:

> [Gen Z] have grown up immersed in a digital-first society marked by severe shifts in economic, environmental and political circumstances. They're the hyper-connected, highly opinionated generation, moved to activism as the internet and social media landscape has made them acutely conscious of and concerned about world events. Having lived in an era of overall progress when it comes to issues like marriage equality and body positivity, they're forging new territory in broader conversations about identity; this is the cohort of gender fluidity and inclusivity in all its forms.[6]

This means that one way for parents to view the fluidity of Gen Z is to think of them in terms of today's most popular social media platforms. Each has its own unique characteristics: YouTube has replaced Facebook as the dominant platform among Gen Zers, not only providing entertainment but also helping shape their perspectives and politics. Snapchat is a place where Gen Z can experiment with their identities and carry on endless conversations. Twitter is the social media megaphone that Gen Z uses to express opinions and hashtag the causes they believe in. TikTok, the zeitgeist of culture, gives Gen Zers the ability to easily upload and share short expressive, humorous, or politically charged videos. Tumblr is a microblogging environment wherein Gen Z can be whatever they want. Last is Instagram, a social networking app that offers Gen Z the opportunity to influence brands, friends, and followers through stories, images, and videos.

Some of these apps and platforms overlap in form and function, but taken as a whole, they allow for far more fluidity online than is feasible in everyday life. In the digital world of Gen Z, divergence is key because it gives them access to limitless expressions.

Second Trait: Significant Creativity

Gen Zers are poised to become the most educated generation of content creators America has ever seen. Demographic research shows that Gen Zers "have higher high school graduation rates and lower dropout rates than those who came before them, and they are more likely to be in college."[7]

From anywhere with a wireless signal, Gen Z can reach the world (or at least anyone with a phone). All you have to do is spend a few minutes on TikTok to see how crazy, funny, and creative Gen Zers can be. They are equally adept at monetizing their efforts through Patreon or GoFundMe to raise support for a cause or a person in need.

In effect, Gen Z represents millions of little businesses being operated from bedrooms around the world.

One of the most prolific Gen Zers today is Kylie Jenner. This twentysomething social media influencer has a personal net worth in the hundreds of millions! Some might say that Jenner's only famous for being famous, but her financial success demonstrates how this generation of digital creators has learned to leverage themselves as a "personal brand." Yet for many Gen Zers, their passion for creativity isn't just about money—it's about expressing themselves in a way that captures their essence and hopefully inspires others.

This was on full display after the 2018 mass shooting at Marjory Stoneman Douglas High School in Parkland, Florida. Before the school shooting, Emma González didn't have a Twitter account. Within days of the massacre, González went to Twitter. In a little over two weeks, she had hundreds of thousands of followers. And now González and her gun-control activist friend and fellow student David Hogg have millions of followers on social media. Together, they are two of the world's leading voices on gun control. (Remember that the first defining trait of Gen Z is "divergent identity"? Well, González now goes by the first name of "X" and uses the gender-neutral pronouns "they/them.")

Here are some questions to consider regarding your own Gen Z kids:

- How connected are your kids to the rest of the world?
- How much of their creativity is on display through the way they interact using technology?
- Are you pretty impressed or disturbed by the huge following your son or daughter has on social media?

Third Trait: Religious Uncertainty

The increased religious disaffection among Gen Z is among the most troubling and unsettling trends affecting this generation—especially for their parents.

Raising kids with a solid biblical footing is a top priority for most Christian parents, and the challenges presented by Gen Z are innumerable. I remember meeting for coffee with a dad who expressed the concerns he and his wife were facing with their recent high school graduate.

Allen, a successful doctor in his late forties, shared with me how hard his son's first year in college had been. At one point in our conversation, Allen expressed something I've heard many times from other parents.

"I just hope that what he learned at a Christian school, and what his mom and I have tried to instill in him through the years, is enough to keep his faith strong in college," Allen said.

Then came the kicker: "But I gotta be honest, Jason. I have my doubts. With all the partying and drinking on college campuses, and the easy access to drugs and hookups, my wife and I worry for our son. And when I say worry, I mean it never goes away. I stay awake sometimes wondering who my son was hanging out with last night."

Social Profile of Gen Z

1. How they think, connect, communicate, and learn is all connected to their smartphone.

2. They are less happy and more hyperactive when spending over four to five hours a day looking at their phones, playing video games, or watching TV.

3. They are more likely than millennials to be "homebodies."

4. They are sheltered and coddled like millennials.

5. They don't get enough sleep.

6. They feel left out and as if their lives don't matter.

7. They are more depressed and contemplate suicide more frequently than previous generations.

8. They are pragmatic when it comes to career choices.

9. They are very involved in activist causes aimed at making a difference.

10. They like to stand up for truth and do the right thing.

I sympathize with parents like Allen. It's tough not to worry about your kids, especially when it seems like almost every day another young person is announcing on social media how he or she recently deconverted from Christianity.

Consider Drew, a typical Gen Zer. Drew was raised in a Christian home. His parents divorced when he was eleven, and as Drew entered his teen years, he developed serious anxiety. He'd sit in church, asking God to help him stop worrying so much. Drew's mother set him up with a counselor, and he received some relief talking through his issues. But the anxiety never really went away. Drew continued to pray, attend church, and visit with his father's family every other weekend. But one day Drew was struck with these thoughts: *Is what I believe even true? I mean, I've prayed and tried to grow in my faith, but none of it seems to matter.*

From that point forward, Drew began to retreat from any activities related to faith. No more church. No more reading the Bible. No more gathering to pray with others. Drew decided that he was no longer a practicing Christian. Drew began constructing his own elaborate system of doubt as he pursued what he called a "spiritual liberation from religious oppressiveness."

Deconversions like Drew's don't always make headlines, but they do leave scars—scars that can last a lifetime. Countless parents have firsthand experience watching their teens and adult children join the growing number of Christian dissenters. And unfortunately, these parents don't always respond in the most helpful ways. They either *overcompensate* for their child's doubts by adding even more religious activities to the family calendar, or (and this is equally detrimental) they *overlook* the crisis of faith because they don't know how to deal with the prospect of a child rejecting Christianity.

If this has been your experience, you are not alone in dealing with the hurt and disappointment. Indeed, Drew's journey might be similar to your own child's story, since nearly half of Gen Zers claim no religious affiliation.[8]

Octavio Esqueda, a professor at Talbot School of Theology at Biola University, writes, "Gen Z were born in a context where religion in general, and Christianity in particular, are no longer a major influence in American culture. The secularization of society has been a trend in the last few years, especially in the Western world, and Gen Z are growing up in this new social context."[9]

Dr. Esqueda's description of Gen Z's shift away from Christianity is the spiritual plight of this generation in America.

With minimal knowledge of Christianity, the Bible, and other religions, Gen Z is perhaps the least religious generation in recent American history. They don't attend church much at all, so they're not familiar with even the most common Christian words and phrases. Most Gen Zers wouldn't know what it means to be "born again" or to "pray the prayer." Try asking them, "What are your spiritual gifts?" or "Are you walking in the Spirit?" You might as well be speaking a foreign language.

Speaking to this very issue, author Rod Dreher has this to say: "American Christians are going to have to come to terms with the brute fact that we live in a culture . . . in which our beliefs make increasingly little sense. We speak a language that the world more and more either cannot hear or finds offensive to its ears."[10]

Truth is, Gen Zers have a hard time subscribing to any particular religion or set of religious beliefs. They don't like labels, and they avoid *exclusive* dogma that challenges moral relativism. Gen Zers see themselves at the center of their own "creative" truth: They are consumed with their own personal experiences, accomplishments, wants, and desires. Many of today's hit songs are about "self." The Gen Z worldview is largely predicated on the raw emotions of the individual.

My friend Dr. Kathy Koch wrote an excellent book for parents titled *Screens and Teens: Connecting with Our Kids in a Wireless World*. In the book, Kathy lays out five self-affirming lies that Gen Z believes about themselves:[11]

Lie No. 1: I am the center of my own universe.
Lie No. 2: I deserve to be happy all the time.
Lie No. 3: I must have choices.
Lie No. 4: I am my own authority.
Lie No. 5: Information is all I need, so I don't need teachers.

These five self-affirming lies have wreaked havoc on the spiritual state of Gen Z. For many Gen Zers, being spiritual isn't about attending religious services, reading the Bible, or participating in group Bible study. To them, pursuing their wants and desires is as important as maintaining a traditional faith that's linked to religious practices and spiritual disciplines. Elizabeth Drescher, author of *Choosing Our Religion*, shares how Gen Z has expanded their definition of *spiritually uplifting activities* to include attending protests or supporting social justice causes.[12]

Simply put, Gen Zers are all over the map when it comes to their views on religion and morality.

Fourth Trait: Sexual Fluidity

Another significant cultural shift within this generational group is the emphasis on affirmation—at least to a point. And nowhere is this more evident than in the area of sexual identity.

After speaking at a church event, I found myself surrounded by a group of high schoolers who shared their thoughts about gender identity and sexuality. In the middle of the conversation, I asked the group, "Who in this group believes gender is binary?" The oldest guy in the group immediately spoke up. "I think gender binary terms are restrictive," he said, "and I don't think I am alone in believing that."

I noticed in the corner of my eye a girl nodding her head in agreement. So I solicited a response from her. To my surprise, she was unwilling to share. Before I could say anything, the teen next to her chimed in, saying, "We need to stop labeling people by the gender they were assigned at birth and start accepting them for who they want to be."

I followed up by asking the group, "So, if *I* believed that gender is binary, what would that say about me?"

The older student shot back, "That you're a Westerner stuck in traditionalism and blinded by your religion."

Unfortunately, what those students shared with me about gender is increasingly supported by Gen Zers. In fact, Gen Z is the first generation to have over half its population buy into the idea that a person's gender is determined not by biology but by how they "identify."

Things are getting so blurred with Gen Zers that almost every traditional notion about sex and gender is being called into question. Consider the following statistics:

- Half of adults ages eighteen to twenty-nine believe it is acceptable to be born one gender yet feel like another.[13]
- One in every eight Gen Zers describes their sexual orientation as something other than heterosexual.[14]
- One in six Gen Z adults identifies as LGBT.[15]

When she was in her early twenties, pop singer Miley Cyrus shared an Instagram post about Tyler Ford, her date to an event. In her post, Miley described Tyler as "a queer, biracial, agender person, whose pronouns are they/them/theirs." In an interview with

Entertainment Tonight, Tyler expressed what "agender" means: "It's pretty simple. I don't identify with a gender. I think I am who I am. I'm a person and that's enough."[16]

The popular dating app Tinder studied nearly 3,500 Gen Zers and found that approximately a third of them had recently "become open to dating different genders."[17]

That's not all. In an effort to accommodate the sexual and gender fluidity among Gen Z, Tinder (in collaboration with the Gay & Lesbian Alliance Against Defamation, also known as GLAAD) "has selected nine initial terms from which people can choose, including Straight, Gay, Lesbian, Bisexual, Asexual, Demisexual, Pansexual, Queer, and Questioning."[18]

Are you surprised?

So, parents, here's my question for you: If your son or daughter (or both) is on Tinder, do you know which categories they clicked to describe themselves on their profile?

Increasing confusion over gender and sexuality will undoubtedly have significant implications on how Gen Z sees themselves and what that means for future marriages and families.

If this sounds bleak, I get it. It sounds that way to me, too. But God is bigger than this. Stick with me here, and we're going to see a light at the end of the tunnel.

Fifth Trait: Ethnic Diversity

How many ethnic groups or nationalities are represented in your family?

Probably quite a few.

Why do I say that? Because Gen Z leads the way as the most ethnically and culturally diverse generation in American history. Gen Z includes a higher percentage of Hispanic, black, Asian, and other ethnic groups than the millennial generation that preceded them.

Take, for example, the Jimenez family. My siblings' and cousins' kids (Gen Zers) represent a broad racial and ethnic makeup. We have Mexican, British, Lebanese, German, and Asian blood—with a dash of Indian. (What would we do without Ancestry.com?)

Another fascinating stat about Gen Z is that 22 percent of them have at least one immigrant parent.[19] This percentage will likely continue to increase in the coming years.

I've been teaching at conferences for years, and I've noticed the increasing diversity among the students. I'm from an ethnically mixed background myself (Hispanic father/white mother) and grew up on the south side of Tucson, Arizona, where a majority of the population was Hispanic and black. I have no problem relating to diverse groups of people from different cultures and backgrounds.

When I consider the cultural and ethnic diversity represented in Gen Z, I view it as an aspect of their beauty. God has created this generation as a representation of our global culture. In fact, most Gen Zers see their race/ethnicity as central to their identity (who they are). This explains why Gen Z is so passionate about their generation's progress in mending racial divides across the American landscape.

Several motivating factors drive this passion. One, as minorities (especially black and Hispanic) continue to increase in number, Gen Z hopes this will reduce racial discrimination. Two, Gen Zers are big proponents of multiculturalism and believe it will decrease segregation and give minorities more opportunities to be seen as equals. Three, increasing ethnic diversity produces fewer ethnocentric families and promotes more interracial relationships, marriages, and families. And four, there is hope that a more diverse population will lead to less racially motivated crime.

Sixth Trait: Progressive Mentality

It won't be long until Generation Z becomes the largest voting bloc in America—one that will (by all estimations) influence our nation's direction for many years to come.

That's a sobering thought, especially considering what we've already learned about Gen Z. Gen Zers have a radically different way of looking at politics. For them, politics isn't about party alliance as much as it's about the issues that are important to them. If a particular candidate speaks to an ideology they are passionate about, they will vote for that candidate regardless of his or her political affiliation.

I saw this firsthand when leading a question-and-answer session with about fifty college students via Zoom. The topic was social issues in American politics, and the majority of the students' questions centered around identity politics. (If you're wondering what *identity politics* means, let me give you a definition from my book *Challenging Conversations*. Identity politics is "the intertwining of discernable overtones ranging from religion to race, ethnicity, sexuality, gender, and even a mentality of victimization."[20])

So there I was, staring at a computer screen filled with fifty little windows—windows containing Gen Zers from different states, backgrounds, and experiences. I quickly learned that most of my students weren't much interested in discussing the US Constitution or the enumerated powers of the federal government. (*Neither am I*, you're probably thinking!) Instead, these students cared much more about why the government isn't doing more for minorities, the LGBT community, and undocumented immigrants.

In light of the situation, I cleared my throat and leaned into my screen to address their concerns.

"I hear you guys," I said, "and thank you for expressing such passion for the less fortunate. Like all of you, I can get upset when I see certain people being overlooked or mistreated. And we do have an obligation as Christians. The Bible clearly states in Proverbs 31:8-9, 'Speak up for those who cannot speak for themselves, for the rights of all who are destitute. Speak up and judge fairly; defend the rights of the poor and needy'" (NIV).

At this point, the voices talking over each other came to a screeching halt. It was actually kind of amusing. The moment I acknowledged their concerns, all the little faces in the little windows started nodding up and down in unison. It was like looking at fifty parrots bobbing their heads at me. I wish I had taken a screenshot of it.

After I breathed a silent sigh of relief, a male student, Matthew, brought up how it feels like there are Planned Parenthood clinics on almost every block of his New Jersey neighborhood. Sounding a bit perturbed by Matthew's comment, a student named Becca interjected, "What does that mean? Planned Parenthood does a lot of good. They provide health services for women, cancer screenings, STD testing, and so much more."

Another student came to Matthew's defense: "Yeah, but you forgot to mention the service Planned Parenthood performs the most. And that is abortions."

I noticed that, based on their body language, several other students were about to unload. I couldn't let this virtual lesson escalate again, so I quickly hit "mute all." (Boy, you gotta love Zoom sometimes!)

I reminded the class that we were not there to debate these issues. They agreed, so I unmuted them and asked this question: "Show of hands. How many of you support Planned Parenthood?" Almost all of them raised their hands except Matthew and a few others.

"Thank you for being honest," I said. "Now, how many of you support a woman's right to have an abortion?"

Again, more than half the group raised their hands. Interesting.

What's ironic to me about Gen Z is that, on average, they are drinking, smoking, and doing drugs less than previous generations. What's more, they apparently don't sleep around as much as their predecessors. Yet they are *more* progressive in their support for legalizing marijuana and same-sex marriage.[21]

Dr. Jean Twenge, professor of psychology at San Diego State University, expounds on the diverse views of Gen Z by pointing out that they are generally more liberal-leaning when it comes to drug legalization, abortion, and the death penalty, while somewhat more conservative on gun rights, national health care, and environmental regulation.[22] And as reported by the Barna Group (in partnership with Impact 360 Institute), most Gen Zers don't believe that marriage should only be between a man and a woman.[23]

Although Dr. Twenge's research shows a slight increase in conservatism among Gen Zers (specifically in supporting traditional marriage, reducing government spending, and protecting First Amendment rights), still well over half of Gen Z's registered voters are motivated by their support for LGBT rights, immigration reform, abortion, universal health care, and welfare reform. And the ballot box isn't the only means by which Gen Zers demonstrate their progressivism. They increasingly engage with and support brands and media organizations that push for change on these political issues.

Seventh Trait: Language Sensitivity

Have you ever said something you thought was innocent yet had one of your kids call you out for your "offensive" language?

I've had plenty of parents tell me troubling stories about how they can't say anything remotely political or even mention someone's hair or skin color without offending their children.

That's because Gen Z is on the warpath to eradicate what they consider to be offensive language. But let me be clear: Such language isn't really about profanity. Based on my experience working with students, Gen Zers are generally more sensitive than millennials when you disagree with them or bring up a controversial topic. Because of their perceived fragility and sensitivity to certain language or topics, some critics have referred to Gen Z as "Generation Snowflake." Name-calling is never beneficial, but I have found that millennials are typically willing to engage with so-called taboo topics. That's not always the case with Gen Z.

For example, I recall a time when I was hanging out with some young Christian students in between classes. I was their guest speaker at a Christian worldview conference, and I had an opportunity to grab a bite and spend some time with them.

When the wide-ranging discussion turned to worship music, one of the students asked, "What say you, Mr. Jimenez? Do you think Christian music has gotten too soft?"

Meanwhile, I had just taken a big bite of my sandwich. As I tried to quickly chew my food, something told me that this seemingly straightforward discussion about music was about to take a wrong turn. I took a gulp of water and looked toward the student who asked the question. As I did, I noticed several nearby students move toward our table to listen in on the conversation.

"To be straight with you," I said, "yes, I do believe that a lot of the music on Christian radio sounds more like romantic songs than worship songs about the attributes of God."

Not sure where this was going, I could feel the palms of my hands starting to sweat. I elaborated on my answer by adding, "I would even say that the Christian music industry has shifted to a more feminine style of worship."

"Oh, *really*?" responded the inquiring student. "Why would you apply the word *feminine* to describe music, as though that's a bad thing? I mean, I used the word *soft* to point out possible weaknesses in Christian music, but you chose a stereotypical description of a certain gender that our generation finds offensive."

Like I said, this was not where I wanted the conversation to go.

We eventually resolved a few things and ended the discussion on a high note (pun intended). I was able to clarify what I meant and to challenge the students on the use of words that have the potential to prompt very different reactions.

Later that night, the conversation about Christian music continued to bother me. *Why do so many young people take things the wrong way?* I wondered. *Why are they so sensitive?*

Looking for answers, I jumped on my computer and tried to learn more about the particular sensitivities of Gen Z. As I perused various articles, I came across a high school student who had openly shared her concerns about how her generation is easily offended. She wrote, "As a member of Generation Z, every day, it feels like society has something new to tiptoe around. Whether that is the language you use or what you post on your social media. It is so hard to keep track of what we can and cannot do anymore, begging a fundamental question: Is Gen Z too sensitive?"[24]

Has growing up within an environment of designated "safe spaces" made Gen Z hypersensitive? More than ever, it feels like genuinely innocent jokes are perceived as insults.

In an online survey of 4,000 students, College Pulse found that more than 40 percent of college students disagree with the First Amendment concept that all speech should be protected, especially when they find it hateful or offensive.[25]

In the age of social media, many Gen Zers feel the need to shut down (or even "cancel") those who say or post anything they consider offensive.

Several years back, a number of undergraduates at Columbia College submitted an essay to the school's newspaper citing how certain topics are "oppressive" and contain "triggering and offensive material that marginalizes student identities in the classroom."[26] These students demanded that the faculty act by providing them with "trigger warnings" before proceeding to teach on aspects of history that might alarm them or cause them to feel uncomfortable due to the presence of microaggressions.

You might be wondering, *What is a microaggression?* According to Merriam-Webster, a microaggression is "a comment or action that subtly and often unconsciously or unintentionally expresses a prejudiced attitude toward a member of a marginalized group (such as a racial minority)."[27]

The problem is that what a Gen Zer might consider as prejudice or a microaggression is often viewed as harmless by someone from a different background or generation. For example, I surveyed a group of high schoolers who believed the following phrases or questions are actually microaggressions:

- "Let the best man win."
- "The most qualified person should get the job."
- "You're very articulate for your age."
- "Where are you from?"
- "Where were you born?"
- "There is only one race—the human race."

In response to requests for trigger warnings and the perceived threat of microaggressions, Alan Levinovitz, an associate professor of religion at James Madison University, writes, "There is a very real danger that these efforts [to institute trigger warnings and safe spaces] will become overzealous and render opposing opinions taboo." Dr. Levinovitz goes on to stress that if free speech is no longer a freedom that professors and college students can exercise, then all conversations about race, gender, and religion will be silenced and replaced with diversity and tolerance training.[28]

As Gen Zers find ever more topics offensive—and seek to stifle free speech and remove certain expressions from their vocabularies, their conversations, their textbooks, and the Internet—there is only one logical outcome: No more healthy debate. No more diversity of thought. A culture that "cancels" dissenting opinions will result in an end to our free and open society.

In their 2018 book *The Coddling of the American Mind*, authors Greg Lukianoff and Jonathan Haidt predict a troubling future for tomorrow's adults: "If we protect children from various classes of potentially upsetting experiences, we make it far more likely that those children will be unable to cope with such events when they leave our protective umbrella."[29]

If you look back at my six statements of alleged microaggressions, I challenge you to find any examples of clear hostility. Will *someone* interpret these (and other) comments as aggressive or insensitive? Probably. It all depends on how, when, and where they grew up, and the family environment in which they were raised. And that is precisely the point! Rather than assume the worst from those who make such comments, why not give them the benefit of the doubt? Unfortunately, that's not the standard response from many members of Gen Z.

In my experience, the increasing tendency for many Gen Zers is to negatively label anyone who commits a single perceived microaggression as insensitive or even outright racist/sexist/homophobic. And yet in making such assessments, Gen Z fails to see their own judgments as acts of aggression.[30] I'm merely making an observation here—I have no desire to argue with Gen Zers over their use of the term *microaggression*. My goal is to better understand their sensitivities. I'll address this topic in more detail in chapter 4.

Eighth Trait: Emotional Instability

So far, we've covered seven traits that characterize Generation Z, but I want to share one final trait that might be the most descriptive of all. I believe the word that best captures the mood of Gen Z is *loneliness*. Whether or not my assessment surprises you, I am certainly not the only one who thinks this way.

After addressing a group of high school students recently at a private Christian school, I met with several members of the faculty. Many of them described how lonely their students felt, even while surrounded by their peers at school. The vice principal herself openly shared that her own two daughters (who grew up at the school) lacked close friendships. A student invited to participate in the discussion told us that he longed to have more meaningful relationships with his peers, and that he'd felt this way throughout his time in high school.

Why is this the case? Why is Gen Z so lonely?

Yes, we can point to their devices and say that has something to do with it. But it goes much deeper than that.

Take divorce, for instance.

Divorce rates among parents raising Gen Z are some of the highest we've ever seen, with baby boomers leading the way in terms of failed marriages.[31] The tendency among Generation X was to marry later in life, divorce sooner, and remarry quicker. Unfortunately for Gen Z, they've experienced more broken relationships early on in life—especially compared with their parents and grandparents—which has forced them to grapple with abandonment issues at an unprecedented rate.

When you consider how overwhelmed they feel, the stresses they face, the increase in cases of depression, and so on, it's easy to understand why Gen Zers are battling loneliness on a scale we've likely never seen before.

I'm no betting man, but I think there's a decent chance that your Gen Z child is struggling with loneliness. I'd be lying if I said my kids have never felt lonely. My wife and I have had many conversations with our children and spent countless hours asking God to deliver them from loneliness. Initiating discussions about loneliness with our kids hasn't always been easy, but it has given us opportunities to share with them how we've dealt with our own loneliness—and the ways that God provided in the end.

Isn't that part of our role as parents—to initiate the tough conversations with our kids and to meet them where they're at?

Now that you've been introduced to Gen Z, in chapter 2 we'll take a closer look at us—the parents tasked with raising this current generation.

Parenting Practice

1. In this introduction to Gen Z, what stood out as something that concerns you? Write it down and pray about it as you continue reading the book.

2. What stood out as something that excites you? Write it down and pray about it as you continue reading the book.

3. Find some time to talk to your kids about their generation. How do your kids feel about the world they are growing up in? What worries them the most? Are they lonely? Why do they think that is? What do your kids see in themselves that you may not see? How confident is your son or daughter about their future?

4. Schedule a time with a few of your friends who also have Gen Z kids. Ask them what they think/know about this generation.

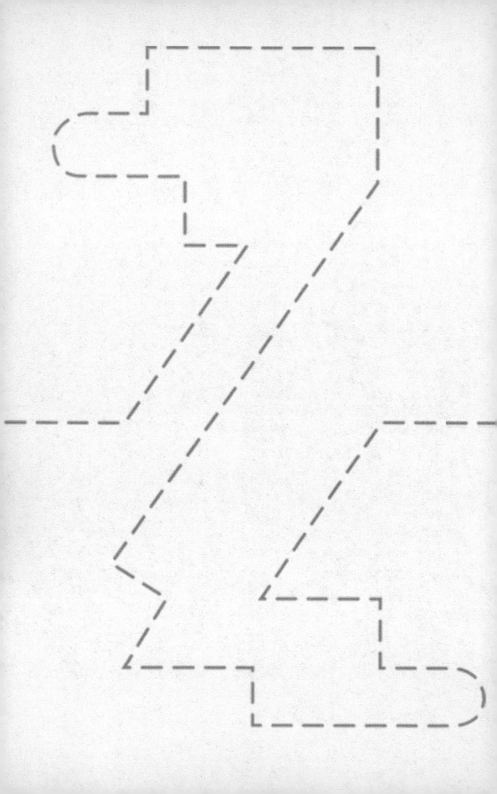

2

A LOOK AT THE PARENTS
RAISING GEN Z

PARENTING BOOKS SOMETIMES get so wrapped up in trying to understand children that they overlook the parents raising them. But ever since your children arrived, you've been the ones who've never stopped loving them, protecting them, and providing for them. I'm talking about all the mothers who took your prenatal vitamins and sang to your child as he or she developed in your womb, and all the fathers who sprang into action to safeguard your new family members.

That was me.

When Tyler, our firstborn, was about to enter the world, I was petrified that the seatbelt wasn't tight enough around his car seat. New to this whole baby thing, I spent nearly two hours tightening and testing to make sure that the belt was fastened nice and snug. At one point, I even ripped (slightly, mind you) the seatbelt because I was pulling on it too hard. Yikes!

We parents take such precautionary steps because nothing means more to us than our kids and their security. We do whatever needs to be done to keep them safe.

Many things have changed since we brought our babies home from the hospital. Looking back, you might even laugh when you think of your concerns as a young parent. *Will she sleep through the night? Is Target still open so I can grab some more diapers?*

I remember a family road trip when Jackson (our third child) was a little over a year old. He was at a stage where he wanted his pacifier *all the time*. And not just any pacifier. No, Jackson only wanted the Soothie Pacifier we had gotten from the hospital. Man, did he love that thing! We tried several other brands to see if he'd use them, but no matter what we gave him, Jackson threw them on the ground and cried for his Soothie. We even bought him new pacifiers that were *identical* (or so we thought) to his blue Soothie.

He wasn't fooled.

So imagine us hitting the road in a van filled with every item you can imagine. When Jackson started to cry, my wife turned around to console him.

"Honey?" my wife said.

"Yeah?" I replied, sensing concern in her voice.

"Where's Jackson's paci?"

The moment she asked, we looked at each other in sheer panic. *What are we going to do? What if Jackson cries for the entire trip? The hotel is eight hours away!*

We quickly located the nearest shopping center and split off into groups searching for a new paci.

In the end, it worked out. Jackson latched on to one of the alternative pacifiers and eventually forgot about his blue Soothie.

Now that Jackson is a teenager, worrying about a pacifier is child's play compared to the issues he faces today. The situations and temptations our kids now face are much more serious, and the sleepless nights for us parents are very real.

— — —

What about you, Mom and Dad? What keeps you up at night? How do you deal with the burdens that weigh down families these days? How are you surviving? *Are you surviving?*

Let's face it—parenting takes its toll. Take the endless emails and texts, trips to the store, unfinished conversations, piles of laundry, and add in the pressures of work and relationships. Who are we kidding—it's hard enough just to get the kids off to school each morning, not to mention feeding the family, going to church, and paying the bills. While you're at it, if you can squeeze in a few precious minutes to decompress and get your mind straight, then good for you!

Your friends are likely no different. Every one of us has drama days of our own. Perhaps it's a friend who's unnerved by the pressures facing her Gen Z son. Maybe it's your buddy who feels like he's not leading his family very well. Or what about learning via Facebook that your friends from church are getting divorced? The reality is that many parents face incredible hardships, yet those same folks resist the urge to let others know how they're feeling and get the help they need.

Parenting is already daunting enough, and that's before we consider the extra challenges involved in raising Generation Z. Families today must confront moral conflicts and societal shifts that previous generations never worried about. Keeping up with Gen Z's ever-changing apps and fads is just one aspect. Considering how many twists and turns parents must navigate in trying to keep up with our kids, it's no wonder that parents raising Gen Zers often feel not just inadequate but shaken to their core.

I repeatedly hear from couples who don't think their parenting is good enough. They tell me how they are constantly dropping the ball with their kids. It can get discouraging, sure, but I remind those moms and dads that it helps to first consider where they're coming from as parents.

In chapter 1 we examined the eight core traits of Gen Z; now it's time to look at the people who are raising Gen Z. Let's turn our focus to us, the adults, in order to better understand why we parent the way we do. Along the way, I'll offer some insights into why so many of us feel inadequate in our parenting.

Right now you might be wondering, *Isn't this book about raising Gen Z? Why are we spending time talking about me?*

If that's the case, then ask yourself, *Who is raising Gen Z? What's the home life like for the typical Gen Zer? What can I learn from other parents who are raising Gen Z? Can they help me be a better parent?*

That's why I'm including this chapter. The truth is that you (and I) have a lot in common with these other parents, yet so often we overlook this. Instead of reaching out to other parents (whether they are younger or older), we keep to ourselves and try to figure out this parenting thing alone.

Gen Z parents are all in the same boat, so why not learn from each other?

After all, why would you want to carry this burden by yourself? That's not good for you or your kids. Furthermore, I believe God can renew your strength and place the right parents in your life at the right time to help ease your burdens and support you when you need prayer, advice, and encouragement.

Trust me when I say this: The more you cultivate relationships with other parents raising Gen Zers, the better equipped you'll be to raise your kids. My wife and I have experienced this firsthand.

We're very thankful for the mature couples and close friendships God has placed in our lives. But it wasn't like the doorbell simply rang one day, and voilà!—there was a gathering of wise Christian couples outside, ready and waiting to be friends and help mentor us. No, it takes a willingness to pursue like-minded parents and hard work to grow and maintain those relationships.

With that in mind, let's take a closer look at the four main categories of parents currently raising Gen Zers. We'll also examine some ways to overcome three flawed methods of parenting often found within these groups.

THE FOUR GROUPS RAISING GENERATION Z

In my office sits the only group photograph ever taken of my grandfather, my father, me, and my son Tyler.

This photo is special for many reasons. For one, it captures four generations of Jimenez men. For another, it makes me smile every time I look at it because it brings back so many beautiful memories. I also get a kick out of how each succeeding generation represented in the picture is a few shades lighter.

If I'm honest, there have also been times when that same picture has brought tears to my eyes. You see, when I was a young father, I rarely asked questions about my grandpa's or my dad's generations. Sure, they told me some stories, and we occasionally reminisced about their childhoods or distant relatives, but that's about it.

Nowadays, as an older—and hopefully a little wiser—dad, I wish I had asked more questions. I wish I knew more about my grandpa's parents and more about his childhood. The same goes for my dad. Thankfully, I can call or FaceTime my father anytime (though he's still trying to figure out his smartphone).

I mention my family because, whether or not you're aware of it, where you came from and the people who raised you likely left a lasting impression on you. For some of you, that impression is positive. For others, it's best forgotten. Yet for good or bad, the people who raised you—their generation—helped make you into the person you are today.

When I consider my grandfather's generation and my father's generation, they seem diametrically opposed, as if someone had drawn a thick dividing line between the two. There was little cross-over or blending.

However, that's not the case today. Since the turn of the century, we've seen a significant intermingling of generations that hasn't taken place before in modern history. Four main parent groups, ranging in age from their late twenties to early sixties, are currently raising Gen Zers. This diversity is astounding!

While there are substantial disparities in age and experience among the parents raising Gen Z, these four groupings also share several commonalities. So as we consider your specific group as well as the other three, try to see yourselves as contemporaries. Don't let your differences intimidate you or put you off. Focus instead on how much you have in common. As you get a better sense of each group, my hope is that you can start bonding with others you know—even cross generationally—and help one another in your parenting.

The following diagram highlights the four groups based on the years they were born. For the sake of this book, I'll refer to them as (1) older Gen X parents, (2) younger Gen X parents, (3) older millennial parents, and (4) younger millennial parents.

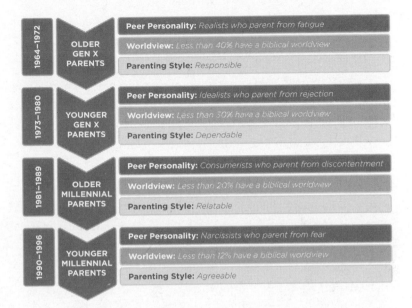

One of the first things you might notice is that the percentage of parents who have a biblical worldview drops significantly with each subsequent group.

You might be wondering, *What's a biblical worldview?*

Good question. Let's start by defining *worldview*. A worldview is like a lens—a lens through which we see and perceive the world. You can think of a worldview as much like a set of tinted glasses. If everyone looks at the same object through green-tinted glasses, they will see it as green. Those looking at the same object through red-tinted glasses will view it as red. That's why people with different worldviews will often interpret the same situation differently.

A more philosophical definition of *worldview* includes existential questions about human origins, identity, morality, and destiny. In other words, your worldview is shaped by whatever you believe to be true about life and how you ought to live your life in the world around you.

Christians, for example, are shaped by a "biblical worldview." Our beliefs about the existential questions of life are grounded in the Bible. We recognize that God's truth illuminates our hearts and minds through the transforming power of God's Holy Spirit. Thus, a Christian who possesses a strong biblical worldview has a solid understanding of doctrinal beliefs, self-identity, and purpose and can engage with nearly all aspects of life and culture.

In addition, you might also notice that as we look at the younger parents, there is an associated seismic shift in parenting styles. Older parents tend to be more authoritarian, religious, and reserved. Younger parents, meanwhile, are less demanding, less religious, and less likely to discipline their children.

Older Gen X Parents (Born 1964–1972)

Larry and Barb are each on their second marriage. Barb is widowed, and Larry is divorced. Larry and Barb grew up during a time when kids largely roamed free, but they've discovered that parenting rules have changed. They try to make church a priority, but Barb's family stopped attending for a while after her husband died, and Larry feels awkward insisting that his stepchildren attend church with the rest of the family.

Larry and Barb's story is quite common among older Gen X parents. You might even say it's the norm.

Following the sexual revolution of the 1960s and '70s, a significant percentage of Gen X parents came from broken homes. When they started families of their own, they tried hard to be responsible parents and provide safe and secure homes for their kids. As realists, they parented their children (mainly millennials) by creating opportunities that made the most sense for their kids.

Many older Gen X parents retain the liberal spirit of their youth but have adopted a conservative, old-fashioned approach to work, finances, and child-rearing. Writing for *Forbes*, market researcher Angela Woo reports that "despite recent studies showing that Gen Xers continue to struggle with debt, some of these studies also show that they aren't too worried about this debt. Even though they are struggling to save for retirement, they are well positioned to become the wealthiest generation—above boomers—within the next few years." She continues, "Roughly half of Gen Xers are financially supporting both a parent and a child at the same time, making financial decisions that can affect all three generations."[1]

> "It's hard keeping track of my kids from my first marriage while trying to be a good mom to my kids with my second husband—and a stepmom to his kids. I'm exhausted most days, and the hard thing is, I still don't feel like I'm doing enough for them."
>
> Elizabeth, 53 years old

Plenty of older Gen Xers are divorced, remarried, or single, and many have had children out of wedlock. Members of this parenting group clearly have a lot on their plates.

A good friend of mine, now in his mid-fifties, has two adult kids from his previous marriage. A few years after he remarried, he and his second wife adopted a baby girl. They also take care of his mother, who has been living with them for several years. I rarely get to see him because he's either working, visiting his older kids, or taking his mom to yet another doctor's appointment.

Despite widespread feelings of regret among this group, older Gen X parents remain dedicated to connecting with their children and helping them grow in their faith.[2] This makes sense considering that older Gen Xers are the most biblically literate of the four parent groups and have made church more of a priority for their families.

Older Gen X parents are less likely to sugarcoat the realities of life for their kids, and they tend to favor a "no-nonsense" approach when it comes to discipline. They are, however, more likely to spoil their children because they didn't have as many luxuries growing up.

Influential Historical Events: Vietnam, *Roe v. Wade*, Watergate scandal, Iran hostage crisis, Mount St. Helens eruption, Chicago Tylenol poisoning deaths.

Younger Gen X Parents (Born 1973–1980)

Justin and Robyn met in college. Robyn had recently broken off a long engagement with her high school sweetheart, and she wasn't ready to jump into another relationship. After some time, Justin convinced Robyn to go out with him. The two soon fell in love, and Justin began pressuring Robyn to sleep with him. This became a sore subject in their relationship. Robyn, a virgin and devout Christian, explained that sex outside marriage is a sin, yet Justin remained undeterred. This went on for a few months until Robyn finally gave in and slept with Justin. Things weren't the same after that.

Justin moved on to a different woman after graduating college and shattered Robyn's dreams of them ever getting married. Robyn eventually met a Christian man named Mike, who had a six-year-old daughter from a previous relationship. Mike and Robyn were married in their church, and their family soon grew. They've now been married for more than twenty years and have five children. They are very active in their church and even teach a marriage class there twice a year.

A large chunk of Gen Zers are being raised by this group of parents—the younger Gen X parents. (This, incidentally, is the segment to which I belong.) We are a generation largely raised by workaholic parents (baby boomers), many of whom either deserted their kids or neglected to provide a stable home. According to the marketing and research firm Reach Advisors, Gen X is one of the "least parented, least nurtured generations in U.S. history."[3]

There are many things I don't particularly like about my grouping. For one, we have a reputation as the original "helicopter parents." In other words, a lot of parents in this segment tend to hover over their children. We tend to be overinvolved and overprotective. We are notoriously preoccupied with making our kids' lives safe and fair and successful and *ideal*—so much so that we are constantly on high alert in case they need us.

The younger Gen X parent group has made it our mission to hand out participation awards for every sporting competition and completely eliminate keeping score. We've pushed for playgrounds with plastic slides and rubber surfaces. The goal is simple: We want to prevent any and all risks to our children, both physically and emotionally. This is the younger Gen Xer's gold standard of parenting.

As a result, younger Gen X parents often work overtime to give their children everything we never had. To do for our kids what no one did for us. I hate to admit it, but we can be insufferable when it comes to our children being noticed. We want others to pay attention. We also expect our institutions (teachers, coaches, administrators) to help our kids perform at their best.

> "My wife and I have a son in college who abandoned the faith several years ago. We still have two kids at home. Every day I pray the Lord gives me the wisdom to lead my family, provide for them, and be more consistent to teach them the Bible."
>
> Robert, 42 years old

Despite these flaws, my generation has a reputation of being dependable, sociable, and committed to teaching our children valuable life lessons.

Influential Historical Events: Challenger shuttle explosion, home video games, fall of the Berlin Wall, Internet, Gulf War, AIDS epidemic, Unabomber.

Older Millennial Parents (Born 1981–1989)

Jessica is a single mother in her mid-thirties raising two rambunctious boys. She's always on the go—whether getting her kids off to school or rushing across town for a meeting. Even after picking the boys up from school, Jessica's day isn't done. There's often another Zoom meeting with her boss, making sure her kids do their homework, then getting them off to soccer or basketball practice. By the time she finally gets the boys to bed, she's exhausted. As Jessica climbs into bed, her phone beeps. It's her ex-husband. *What does he want this late at night?* Afraid to look, Jessica puts her phone on the charger and turns out the lights.

Alone in the dark, she starts to pray, "Heavenly Father, please take care of my boys. Give me the patience, love, and energy to be the best mom I can be for them. I also pray they never end up like their father. Please give me the strength I need for tomorrow. Please help me not to worry about the bills or the problems I'm having at work." After asking for patience to deal with her ex, Jessica closes her eyes. She hopes to get at least five hours of sleep before the alarm goes off and she gets to do it all over again tomorrow.

Although parents in every segment are busier than ever, older millennial parents generally spend more time with their kids than the other three parent groups. According to Boston College's Center for Work and Family, "Millennial fathers are more enthusiastic about parenting duties than dads of previous generations. In fact, many millennial families, especially those with two working parents, embrace a 'co-parenting' approach, in which responsibilities for all things kid-related are split more or less equally between both parents."[4]

A particular issue with this group of parents is their tendency to post their dirty laundry on social media. Other times, they portray an idealized version of their lives online. Many have admitted that they sometimes become so preoccupied with posting, tweeting, and commenting that they neglect some of their responsibilities at home.

Another major shift among younger Gen X parents and older millennial parents is the restructuring of the family. Millennial parents in general typically marry later in life than previous generations and are having fewer children than baby boomers and Gen X. According to the US Census Bureau, "Married couples comprise 68% of parents in the 21st century, compared to 93% in the 1950s."[5]

> "With sports on Sundays and travel games every other weekend, it's been forever since our family has been to church. I still keep up with a few friends from church, but I don't have Christian community that encourages me and helps me be a better wife and mother."
>
> Tammy, 35 years old

Research published by Princeton University shows just how diverse familial status is among this group of parents: "As of 2017, between 2 million and 3.7 million children under age 18 had an LGBT parent, and approximately 200,000 of them were being raised by a same-sex couple. Many of these children were being raised by a single LGBT parent or by a different-sex couple where one parent was bisexual."[6]

Even within these varied family structures, a primary emphasis among these parents is to better relate to their children. Many older millennials were raised by strict parents and brought up in authoritarian homes, but that's not the way they want to parent their children. They prefer to shape their Gen Z kids through positivity and encouragement, not strict discipline.

Influential Historical Events: Rodney King riots, O. J. Simpson trial, death of Princess Diana, impeachment of Bill Clinton.

Younger Millennial Parents (Born 1990–1996)

Ben and Christina are a young, vibrant couple who are passionate about their faith, their adorable twins, and the great outdoors. But as their kids got older, the family struggled to find the right church home. One particular location seemed promising—the pastor was cordial, and he taught from the Bible. The music, on the other hand, sometimes seemed more like a concert than a worship service. Ben and Christina preferred a more liturgical and reflective style, but their kids seemed to be settling in. So Ben and Christina joined a midweek discipleship group.

Months later, however, Ben and Christina were still struggling. They hadn't made any close friends, and they found it hard to keep up with all the activities at the church. Deep down, this young couple just wanted to belong. Ben and Christina quietly hoped for a few older couples to take them under their wings, disciple them, and offer parental guidance, but that never happened. A short time later, COVID-19 hit, and the church started streaming services online. When the building reopened, Ben and Christina didn't go back. They decided that corporate worship wasn't for them. They preferred streaming church services online, listening to popular Christian podcasts, and watching a sermon or two on YouTube whenever they had a chance.

In general, younger millennial parents are inclined to embrace gender-neutral parenting, and (similar to older millennials) these twenty- and thirtysomethings prefer a more agreeable approach with their kids—one in which they act less like disciplinarians and more like friends.

Younger millennial parents are often more comfortable negotiating with their kids instead of telling them what to do. They seek minimal input from their friends regarding parenting and would rather play the "friend" role than the "parent" role with their kids. A quick fix for them is to hop on YouTube in search of parenting advice. Of particular concern among young millennial parents are rising costs and stagnant wages. Many of them worry about finances while striving to put aside money for their kids' college tuition.

> *"I'm a single mom with an eight-year-old boy. My boyfriend left me for another woman. This past year I had to move back in with my mom and my stepdad so I can save up some money. I never thought I'd end up like this, but I'm trying to remain strong for my son."*
>
> Leah, 26 years old

Even more than their predecessors, this group of parents is plagued by anxiety and fear. I can't tell you how many conversations I've had with millennial parents who worry about their children's safety, health, and plans for the future.

At a recent retreat for parents organized by my church, a young millennial father sat down at my table. He didn't say much at first, but once the other parents left, he cleared his throat rather awkwardly and said, "Do you mind if I ask you a few questions?"

"Sure, Christopher," I replied. "What's up?"

"Well, I haven't talked to anybody about this, but when I saw you, I felt like you would be a good person to talk to."

"I'm glad you did, Christopher," I reassured him. "And thank you for trusting me with whatever you're going through."

That seemed to put Christopher more at ease.

"Um, okay," he started. "How should I say this? It's about my wife. She's totally consumed with social media. I mean, to the point where she's constantly checking her phone, posting about what's wrong with the world—stuff like that. I even had a buddy send me a screenshot of my wife's harsh comment on one of his posts. I've tried talking to her, but it always leads to us arguing. I don't know what else to do."

Before I could say anything, Christopher got his second wind: "But what I'm most concerned about is how much anxiety my wife has about our kids. She's always checking on them, and most of the time she won't let them do anything because she's afraid that they're going to get hurt."

I encouraged Christopher to be more proactive in leading his family spiritually, and I suggested that he and his wife set aside more time for praying together as a couple. It was also clear that Christopher and his wife needed to invest in biblical community. We looked at Titus 2 together, and I shared with him the importance of having mentors—especially as a married couple.

Christopher was totally on board and couldn't wait to get started.

I've had many conversations with parents just like the one I had with Christopher. He's not alone—this demographic carries a lot of anxiety, and it spills over to their kids. Bottom line, it isn't healthy.

Despite the worries of so many millennial parents, one thing that has impressed me is the willingness of so many to put their kids ahead of their careers. It doesn't happen right away—many younger millennial parents are still self-absorbed—but signs indicate that as they get older, they tend to prioritize family life and take on more responsibility.[7]

Influential Historical Events: Y2K scare, 9/11 terrorist attacks, iPhone debut, Facebook launch, Enron corporate fraud scandal, stock market crash, war on terror, Hurricane Katrina, 2007–2009 recession, Bernie Madoff Ponzi scheme.

In the next chapter, we'll learn about different parenting styles. I'll provide help for parents who need to confront their insecurities and let go of anything that is holding them back from being the best parents they can be.

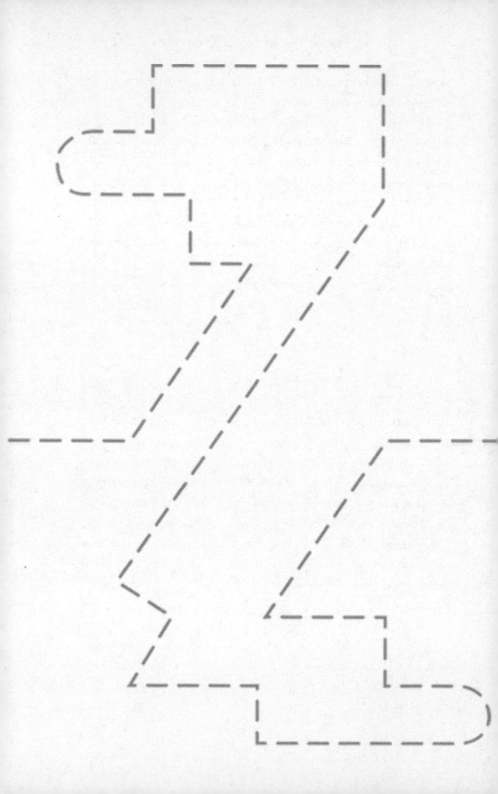

3

THREE PARENTING FLAWS AFFECTING GEN Z

AROUND 2008, THE CONCEPT of "free-range parenting" began to gain popularity. The term was new, but the concept wasn't. Advocates of free-range parenting proposed that children deserve some unsupervised time to play, explore, and be, well, kids. In other words, kids don't need to be hovered over every minute of every day—essentially the opposite of "helicopter parenting." Opponents argued that safety concerns overrode the need for freedom, and the "free-range" concept ultimately received mixed reviews.

One camp of parents is involved in almost every aspect of their children's lives. Their kids can't do much of anything without parental consent. In the other camp are the "free-range" parents who give their kids space and freedom. For example, they're allowed to walk home alone from school or the park once they reach a certain age.

There's certainly a tendency to polarize parenting into opposing extremes, but as you probably know, rarely do extremes represent good parenting. We need to find a proper balance. As you reflect on the four parental age groups from the previous chapter, you can see that finding the proper balance as a parent isn't always easy.

In chapter 8 I'll address some standards of biblical parenting, and in chapter 9 I'll talk about how to exercise your authority as a parent or stepparent. But for now, let's address three flawed parenting approaches that affect Gen Z to some degree. I'm not suggesting that we as parents are responsible for every mistake our kids make, but the mistakes we commit as parents can, and often do, affect our children. A misguided parenting style can prompt kids to act out in defiant and reckless ways.

Let's begin with the chart below. The shaded boxes at the top are the three flawed parenting styles, and beneath each is a key failure of that approach. The bottom three boxes in each column are characteristics often seen in children raised under that style.

CONTROL PARENTING	PARANOID PARENTING	DETACHED PARENTING
Failure to Prepare	Failure to Release	Failure to Provide
Oppressive	Obsessive	Oblivious
Wired to Interfere	Controlled by Fear	Geared to Ignore
Creates Conflict	Avoids Conflict	Disregards Conflict

After giving it some thought, note which flawed parenting approach you tend to struggle with the most. Do your best to explain why you think that is.

My flawed parenting approach is _____.

_____

_____

_____

_____

Identifying your flawed parenting approach isn't supposed to make you feel like a failure. It's just a way to help you understand your primary or default method of parenting. You might feel like you don't belong entirely in one box, and that's certainly possible. The key to this exercise is for you to be straightforward and honest with yourself. My goal is to help you grasp some of the reasons why you might parent this way, while also offering some biblical guidance on overcoming your shortcomings as a parent. (We all have them!)

Referring back to the diagram in chapter 2 summarizing the four parental age groups, you'll notice that very few millennial parents have a biblical worldview. As a matter of fact, Gen X and millennials in general have weaker biblical worldviews than previous generations. That shift has led to some major flaws when it comes to raising kids. If our parenting is characterized by control, fear, or absence, it will have major implications for our children. And this is more likely to happen when parents lack a robust biblical worldview.

Of course, spiritual and biblical maturity is not the sole measure of a parent's flaws or abilities. If you're a Gen X parent (like me), I think you might agree that our generation's way of parenting is just as messed up as those of prior generations—as well as subsequent ones! Keep in mind that Gen X earned the notorious label of "the Neglected Generation."

This chapter isn't a contest about which parents are better or worse. It's about recognizing three common, yet flawed, parenting approaches that are widespread across generations, then determining how we can best overcome them by relying on the wisdom of Scripture.

But before we proceed any further, I want to say something important: No parent on the planet has it all together. Raising kids isn't easy. There will be times when even the most highly recommended strategy or parenting method will fail. But our focus isn't on being *perfect* parents, nor is it our goal to raise *well-behaved* kids. The goal is for you to *be the parent that your kids need.*

Our tendency is to look back at all our failed attempts to be the best parents and wonder if things can or ever will change. But that's the wrong question. As we examine these three flawed parenting approaches, I encourage you to be open to God's correction in certain areas of your parenting and allow Him to redirect your steps. A humble heart will not be helpful just to you but to your kids as well. And if you're feeling overwhelmed by the demands of parenting, not to mention tired of monitoring your children's every move, then begin by looking to God for help. Ask Him to renew your strength.

THE CONTROLLING PARENT

If you struggle with anger, are uncomfortable with emotional intimacy, or don't like being corrected, then there's a strong chance that you have the tendencies of a "controlling" parent. Controlling parents are typically strong-willed, strict, and overbearing, yet they have also mastered the ability to mask their emotions. In many cases, these tendencies arise from childhood trauma—often *unrecognized* trauma. Childhood trauma explains (to some extent) why controlling parents have a hard time letting their guard down. Especially if you learned (implicitly or explicitly) to detach yourself from the traumatic events of your past, it's likely that you have never fully recognized their impact. Thus, for controlling parents, it's easier to bark orders than it is to warm up to people. Being in control gives you a sense of strength and offers protection from feelings of vulnerability and insecurity.

Advice for Controlling Parents: Stop Thinking You Always Know What's Best

There's no gentle way to say this, so I'll just put it out there: The measure of a good parent *isn't* someone who controls his or her kids and deprives them of making decisions for themselves.

There's a tendency for controlling parents to think that they always know best. However, there's a big difference between *knowing what's best* for your kids and *thinking you know what's best* for them. You might really want the best for your children, but that doesn't mean you always do the best thing for them.

What *is* best for you and your kids is that you stop trying to control every aspect of their lives from the moment they wake up to the time they go to bed. First, it's an impossible burden. Only God is in control of all things—not you, not me. None of us can fully direct the thoughts and actions of our children. We can't make them behave exactly the way we want. Second, we need to acknowledge our dependence on God: "Not that we are sufficient in ourselves to claim anything as coming from us, but our sufficiency is from God" (2 Corinthians 3:5).

There's a guy I know—let's call him Jim—who is a control freak. When Jim signed up his kids for youth sports, he spent big money on trainers and home equipment to help improve his children's performance. One time I asked Jim if his kids really love playing sports. (I asked him this question because his children aren't particularly good at sports.) Even Jim's wife told me that she didn't think it was good to push them so hard at something they didn't like. Jim's response was typical of the classic controlling father: "I know what I'm doing for my kids. I would have killed to have what I've been able to give my kids. They may not like it now, but I promise you it will pay off in the end."

You want to admire Jim's desire to help his children. He's very passionate and driven to make his kids' lives a success, but to what end? It's great that Jim is involved with his children and is willing to put in time, money, and effort for his kids. Those are great qualities, but they are also the qualities common among controlling parents. In Jim's case, his controlling nature isn't actually helping his kids. He's turned into a micromanaging ruler rather than a dad who simply loves his kids for who they are.

The fact that Jim's wife and kids don't think sports are a priority ought to be enough for Jim to loosen his grip and start listening to his family. It ought to be, but it doesn't always work that way. How you guide your kids and interact with them speaks to the intentions of your heart. Most parents *want* to be more patient and less demanding. They *don't want* to freak out when things don't happen the way they planned. But changing ingrained habits takes time, and we begin by asking the Holy Spirit to soften our hearts.

Your job as a parent is not to *control* your kids. Your job is to *lead* them. To *guide* them. You can establish standards for your kids without being controlling. You can set boundaries and reasonable expectations without impeding their freedom. A good counselor friend of mine says it this way: "Parent your kids with strength, but remain flexible."

Ask God to examine your heart. Own up to your pride and demonstrate to your kids that you will trust the path God has for them. It's a powerful example when your children see you acknowledge your mistakes. It's even better when they see you work to correct them.

If you take away just one point from this section, let it be this: Your children need a parent, not a dictator. Support them with increasing freedoms that match their maturity levels, and allow them to take on more age-appropriate responsibilities to earn your trust. (We'll talk more about this in chapter 9.)

Finally, meditate on 1 Peter 5:6-7: "Humble yourselves, therefore, under the mighty hand of God so that at the proper time he may exalt you, casting all your anxieties on him, because he cares for you."

THE PARANOID PARENT

"So, let me get this right," I said, with a bit of sarcasm in my voice. "You're not letting your son get his driver's license because there are too many crazy drivers out there?"

"Absolutely!" the mother insisted. "My job is to protect my son, and I'm not going to send him out there on his own when there are so many stories about road rage—not to mention all the careless people looking at their phones while driving."

The intensity of her voice made it clear that a brief conversation probably wouldn't resolve her concerns. I had another conference session to speak at, but I didn't want to send her on her way without acknowledging her feelings.

"You're right," I replied. "There *are* a lot of crazy drivers out there. And I know you believe that what you're doing for your son is for his own good. But, if I may, at what cost?"

"What do you mean?" she replied, with more than a hint of annoyance in her voice.

"Well, let me ask you this: Does your son want to drive? Does he want you to give him more freedom and allow him to take risks and make mistakes?"

"Well, yeah. But—"

"But nothing," I quickly interjected. "By being so worried about your son's safety, it's costing you your standing with him as a safe person your son can come to when he needs you. And I'm sure you don't want that, right?"

At this point, the now-silent mother reached into her purse for a tissue.

"Besides, what about *your* health? I'm guessing that this paranoia about your son's safety has become way too stressful for you?"

"You're right," she said as she wiped her eyes. "I've got high blood pressure, and my anxiety has taken its toll on my health."

Are you like this mom? Have you ever let fears about your children's security and well-being overwhelm you? If so, there's a decent chance that you are an alarmist who struggles with paranoia and anxiety—and, in many cases, abandonment issues.

Paranoid parents have difficulty coping with social pressures, trusting people, and avoiding unhealthy codependency in their relationships. As a direct consequence, they find themselves constantly monitoring their kids and limiting their freedoms out of concern that something terrible might happen. Thoughts such as *What will I do if something bad happens to my kids?* are a constant among paranoid parents.

Advice for Paranoid Parents: Exchange Your Fear for Faith in God

Being concerned for our children seems like a key part of the parental job description—to care about their well-being and do everything in our power to keep them safe. And I firmly believe that this is exactly what most parents who struggle with fear and paranoia are trying to do. But while that's sometimes commendable, it's not always recommended. When your paranoia prompts you to put your kids into lockdown mode, you've almost certainly gone too far. You can't allow your fears of the world to make you dictate your child's every move or lack thereof. It's not healthy for you or your child.

Sure, you can justify your behavior as simply that of a "concerned" parent. But who are we kidding? Being "concerned" doesn't mean we should fit our kids with ankle monitors—or, even worse, to never let them leave the house. There's a considerable difference between being *concerned* and being *overprotective*.

Moreover, your fears and anxieties will inevitably spill over into your other relationships. When your friends, family, and other loved ones see your angst, what message do you think that sends? How are you modeling faith to others around you if you let fear dominate your life (see Isaiah 41:10)?

Just because the world can be dangerous doesn't mean we automatically assume the worst and never let our children out of our sight.

I recall meeting a couple in their late sixties who told me about the tragic death of their daughter in a car accident. The mother described how, after losing their daughter, she wouldn't risk letting her other children drive themselves to school. For the next several years, she personally drove them where they needed to go. It was hard to hear but understandable.

Other parents have suffered through traumatic illnesses or other agonizing setbacks with their children that have caused them to become anxious or fearful.

Suffering is undeniable and often unavoidable. Whether it is the loss of a loved one, a traumatic experience, or severe emotional or physical pain, no one is immune from the hurts of this life. And because life is filled with so many risks and unknowns, it's in our best interests to lean on and trust the Lord by giving Him our pain and our fears.

If you want your child to both survive *and* thrive in this world, you need to trust that God will watch over them. (We will cover this in more detail in chapter 12.)

As you learn to give your fears to the Lord, you will begin

to experience a peace like no other. Not only will your thoughts change for the better, but you'll develop a better attitude and a whole new approach to parenting—faith over fear.

In his book *Christian Counseling: A Comprehensive Guide*, Dr. Gary Collins says this about dealing with fear:

> The Bible does not say there is anything wrong with facing anxious situations honestly or with using our God-given brains to find ways for dealing with the identifiable problems of life. To ignore danger is foolish and wrong. Christians can move forward with confidence, especially if they commit their actions to God and seek his guidance. But it is wrong, and unhealthy, to be immobilized by excessive worry. Our persisting concerns must be committed in prayer to God, who, sometimes working through Christian counselors, can release us from paralyzing fear or anxiety and can free us to deal realistically with the needs and welfare both of others and of ourselves.[1]

Be honest with your kids. Let them know that you struggle with fear. But also tell them that you don't want fear to interfere with how you raise them.

As you open up to your family, allow them to be a part of your healing process. Ask for their prayers and look for moments to share with them that will help give all of you peace of mind. Here are some ways to reduce paranoia in your life:

1. Confess your fears to God and ask Him daily to provide the faith you need to be an overcomer (1 John 5:4-5).
2. Seek help from your spouse, a trusted friend, or perhaps a Christian counselor to help you work through your fears.

3. Make a list of Bible verses to recite and pray through when you experience fearful thoughts or feelings of anxiety. Here's a few to get you started: Psalm 94:19; Matthew 6:34; John 14:27; 1 Peter 5:7. Paul writes in Philippians 4:6: "Do not be anxious about anything, but in everything by prayer and supplication with thanksgiving let your requests be made known to God."

4. Look for ways to relate to your child. You might say, "I want you to know that I have your best interests at heart. I know I can act paranoid at times, and it might seem like I don't trust you. But I do. So I'm sorry for allowing fear to keep me from believing in you and withholding freedoms that you have earned. I hope you will forgive me."

5. Never forget this tremendous promise spoken by Jesus: "Peace I leave with you; my peace I give to you. Not as the world gives do I give to you. Let not your hearts be troubled, neither let them be afraid" (John 14:27).

THE DETACHED PARENT

Mandy is a mother of six. She has difficulty demonstrating affection to her kids, and she knows it. She wrote to my organization (Stand Strong Ministries) seeking help. Here's a part of what she said: "As an emotionally unstable mother, I can't tell you how hard it is for me to show affection to my children. I don't even like being around people displaying affection. It makes me feel uncomfortable. I hate feeling this way and blame my parents, who never told me they loved me."

Can you relate to Mandy's situation? If so, you might have some characteristics of a "detached parent." Here's the unfortunate truth: Most parents I have counseled who have detachment issues also experienced some sort of neglect or abuse as a child. This could very well be your story. And if it is, I am deeply sorry. Other detached parents attribute their feelings to a lack of stability in their childhood home, often related to infidelity, divorce, or excessive conflict in their parents' marriage.

Derek, the father of a tween boy, shared with me that he made note of every broken promise his dad and mom had made when he was a kid. He also shared how, when he was an adult, a counselor helped him realize that his parents had neglected him. Derek had never seen it that way—he thought they were just too busy doing adult things. But his counselor's reasoning made sense, and it explained why Derek had ongoing trust issues and was emotionally disconnected from his son.

Advice for Detached Parents: Open Up to God and Start Fresh (and Consider Seeking Professional Help)

Detached parents frequently come off as irritable and self-centered, and they tend to disengage when things become emotionally charged. But finding it difficult to express your emotions or having a hard time showing affection doesn't mean you don't love your kids. Those are lies from Satan. In those moments of doubt, such as when you struggle to connect with your child, it's important to share those doubts with God in prayer, perhaps by writing in a prayer journal. You might be skeptical about journaling, but it's a great exercise to help you process your thoughts and emotions.

I also recommend that parents with detachment issues consider seeing a qualified Christian counselor. A counselor can help you work through any deep-seated pain stemming from your childhood. A counselor can also help by recommending ways to engage emotionally with your children—ways that can bring healing to your family.

Start working on small ways to communicate love to your kids. If hugging is too awkward for you at first, then begin by giving your son or daughter a gentle pat on the back. If you struggle with verbally expressing your feelings, try writing notes of affirmation and leaving them on your child's bed. Start making an everyday habit of telling your kids "I love you." I understand that this might be hard for you, especially at first. But don't withhold love from your kids just because your mother or father never demonstrated their love for you. That wasn't your fault, and it's certainly not your children's fault.

Kids are resilient and typically very forgiving. So at some point, as you take small steps toward showing affection, let them know that you are trying (with God's help) to be more personal and encouraging, and that you want to help them grow spiritually too.

One last thing—if you happen to have an affectionate child, try hard not to avoid their touch. Let your children help *you* become more like them. Just the other day, I was sitting at the kitchen table after dinner talking with my wife. My son Jackson came up behind me, and as he bent down to hug me, we bumped heads. In the moment, I was upset at him for interrupting our conversation and knocking my glasses off my face. With annoyance in my voice, I said to Jackson, "Buddy, you can't just randomly come up behind someone and give them a hug when they least expect it."

My son walked away defeated. I knew right away that I'd made a mistake, so I got up from my chair and headed immediately to Jackson's room. I told him I was sorry for speaking to him like that, and I asked for his forgiveness. I then expressed how much I loved his hugs and asked if I could give him one.

Your children don't need you to be someone you're not. They need you to be the parent God made you to be. For them.

— — —

Take some time to identify the approach that most applies to you (controlling parent, paranoid parent, or detached parent) and follow the suggested advice every day for three weeks. Take note of any changes you see in your kids.

If you're married, find an older married couple willing to disciple you and your spouse. If you're a single parent, find a mature Christian willing to disciple you. Be open with them about your parenting flaws and allow them to help you work through your struggles and shortcomings.

Parenting Practice

1. Find a time each day to share with God your innermost pain. Don't hold back. Express to Him why you feel a certain way, or why you don't feel much of anything. Meditate on the promise of Psalm 34:18: "The LORD is near to the brokenhearted and saves the crushed in spirit."

2. Don't brush off the damage that emotional unavailability might have on your children. Making yourself emotionally available can help prevent all sorts of insecurities throughout their teen years.

3. Consider having yourself and your family meet with a pastor to see what kind of support your church can offer. They might also help in recommending a family therapist. Please don't view this as a negative assessment of you. View it as an answer to prayer—an opportunity to have a qualified individual help you work through your emotional problems.

4. Monitor how much time you spend online and be careful what you post. Try to avoid obsessing over what others think of you, lest it might cause you to neglect your responsibilities at home. Seeing other families' "ideal lives" on social media can also cause you to think less positively of your own situation. (And don't assume those picture-perfect social media profiles represent the whole truth about their daily lives!)

5. Don't use "stuff" to compensate for not being there for your kids. Your kids don't need a new iPhone or free rein to watch whatever they want on Netflix. Your kids need you! They need hugs and kisses, the words "I love you," and time together to laugh and cry. Simply put, *show* your kids how much you care for them.

PART TWO

CONCERNS FACING
GEN Z

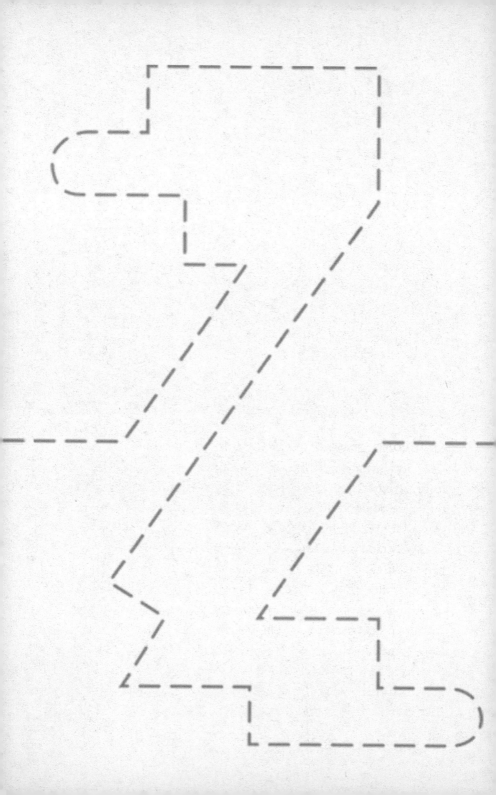

4

DIGITAL OBSESSION AND ITS DANGEROUS EFFECTS

I COULDN'T BELIEVE MY EYES.

It happened one evening when my wife received a last-minute request from a realtor to show our house. We needed to be out of the house, so I told the family to jump in the van because we were going out to eat. I didn't need to tell them twice.

As my family and I were shown to our seats, I noticed another family dining at a nearby table. I was struck by the fact that every single family member (except the mother) had headphones on. Every single one of them was staring at a mobile device. Completely sucked in. One kid was watching a movie, another was playing a video game, and the dad had on a pair of humongous headphones connected to his iPad as he took in a soccer match. Meanwhile, his wife just looked at her family. She was clearly agitated as she pecked at her food in silence.

I really wanted to say something. My wife, in her wisdom, advised against it.

I couldn't sleep that night. The image of that family at the restaurant lingered in my mind. *What is their home life like? What kind of influence do the parents have over their kids, if any? How addicted are they to their devices?*

The story was the same in Hilton Head, South Carolina. My wife and I were enjoying a nice breakfast at a French bakery. I looked around the establishment and noticed a millennial couple completely occupied with their phones. Neither one of them spoke a word to the other.

I glanced over at another table, where a family had propped up an iPad for their toddler to watch a movie—the volume loud enough for the whole place to hear—while Mom took small bites with one hand and kept the other one free to scroll through the smartphone sitting on the table.

To get my mind off all this digital obsession, I reached for a sip of cold water. But my glass was empty. I looked for our waiter. At first I couldn't find him. When I finally spotted him, he was in the back of the bakery, leaning against the wall. Yep, you guessed it—he was busy texting on his phone.

What has happened to us?

HOW GEN Z IS AFFECTED

Hardwired by Tech

Could you imagine growing up in the 1980s or early 1990s and carrying around a handheld phone or computer worth anywhere from $500 to $1,000?

No way, dude! (Sorry, I needed to relive my childhood for a moment.)

When I was in high school, I remember seeing a Toshiba ad for their latest laptop computers. I didn't know anyone who owned a laptop, and I thought it would be incredibly cool to have one. The following week, I bought a new Toshiba laptop for a ridiculous amount of money.

Except for my car, it was the most expensive thing I had ever purchased. I brought it to school the very next day. As the other students pulled notebooks out of their backpacks, I got out my two-inch-thick laptop. It seemed like the entire class gathered around my desk to check out my nifty new toy, which incidentally came preloaded with two music videos: "Two Princes" by Spin Doctors and Gloria Estefan's "Get on Your Feet." (Yes, I am once again dating myself.) After that, all my friends wanted to ditch their parents' typewriters and buy laptops of their own. One friend in class blurted out, "Where do you even get one of those things?"

That was then. Nowadays, carrying around the latest smartphone, smartwatch, or laptop is no longer a big deal. It's *expected*.

Whether it's an iPad used to keep a toddler occupied or a phone used to keep in constant contact with the outside world, digital devices are not so much tools for Gen Z to use as they are virtual extensions of their bodies. As one student told me, "I break out in a panic if I don't have my phone with me." Another one said, "The first thing I do when I wake up is to check my phone."

Having a device in their hands is all Gen Z has ever known. They have grown up downloading games, streaming movies, and posting pics. If Gen Zers want to express their beliefs, record a song, produce a video, or self-publish a book, they can. Technology makes it possible. Back in the day, we got our news from two or three main outlets. Now kids develop their belief systems from music, YouTube videos, social media posts, comments, retweets, and streaming services like Netflix, Discovery+, and Amazon Prime.

Two of my friends, Sean McDowell and Jim Wallace, make an interesting point in their book *So the Next Generation Will Know*: "While Millennials were raised on smartphones, only Gen Z was raised by parents (Gen X and Millennials) who were *also* on smartphones. The use of digital technology—and in particular social media—is perhaps the defining characteristic of this generation."[1]

And most parents don't want to fight about it. One father of Gen Zers told me, "It's not like I endorse phones at the dinner table. It's just that phones are a part of our lives, and we've just got to accept it." (What he really meant was, *I've set a bad example for my kids, and I have no clue how to redeem the situation.*)

It's pretty nifty that Gen Z can ask Alexa or Google to name that tune or explain how to boil an egg. But it's unbelievably scary to think of the limitless access our Gen Z kids have to whatever information is out there. It makes you wonder—what will be the side effects of too much screen time down the road?

An Eight-Second Attention Span

Have you ever heard of an *elevator pitch*? If you're not familiar with the term, an elevator pitch (or speech) is a brief yet compelling way to describe something. The idea is that you should be able to sum up who you are or what your company does in the short time span of an elevator ride. Hence the name.

I bring up the concept of an elevator pitch because today's typical tweens and teens have an attention span of approximately eight seconds.[2] That's *eight seconds*, parents! What can you get into a young person's head in eight measly seconds? Not much.

Not long ago, my wife and I had a few friends over for dinner to discuss parenting our Gen Z kids. One of the dads shared with the group how hard it is for him to get his children's attention when they are on their phones. He said it's a battle to get them to even acknowledge what he just said to them. That father's experience resonated with all of us. His wife spoke up next: "We also have a hard time trusting that our kids will remember to do what we told them to do." At this point, the whole group of parents chimed in to express their own frustrations and concerns over this same issue.

We all agreed that Gen Zers have an uncanny ability to send and receive texts at all hours— day or night. Social media saturation means that Gen Z is easily distracted and often finds it difficult to focus on things that really matter. Moreover, they tend to communicate in small, "bite-size" morsels of information.[4] This doesn't apply to every member of Gen Z, of course, but I know many Gen Zers who struggle to find real depth and meaning in their conversations.

> *Common Sense Media reports that the average daily media use of tweens (eight to twelve years old) is over five hours, and the average for teens (thirteen to eighteen years old) is more than eight hours. And that's excluding the amount of time they use media for school.*[3]

One reason is that many Gen Zers are *overexposed* to information yet *underexposed* to real-life experiences. Author Tim Elmore refers to this phenomenon as "artificial maturity."[5] And in their book *Generation Z Unfiltered*, Tim Elmore and Andrew McPeak list three consequences of artificial maturity in young people:

1. They can act immature or be paranoid due to little experience.
2. They can act without discretion since privacy allows for it.
3. They can drift into amoralism—assuming no ethical boundaries.[6]

Artificial maturity is no joke. I see it all the time when working with Gen Zers. I noticed it in a message I received from an eighteen-year-old via Facebook: "If it were up to me, I would never meet with people in person," he wrote. "I prefer doing everything over text, FaceTime, or Google Meet."

Another example of artificial maturity is when a child won't pay attention to his or her parents for any length of time. Or when tweens or teens can't seem to focus on a project for more than five minutes because they are constantly checking their phones.

You'd think that the sheer amount of information Gen Z processes every day would increase their knowledge. Not so. Think of your child's brain as a computer. What happens when you run too many programs on your computer simultaneously? The computer's processor starts to slow down. The same thing applies when your kid's brain is trying to download too much information: It can only take so much. Especially if your child is accessing information that is beyond their emotional and mental maturity level.

"More than half of teens and young adults . . . (53%) say they put off or procrastinate doing homework or other things because of technology. They also blame technology for feeling more distracted (50%) and less productive (36%), for wasting a lot of time (54%) and for shortening their attention span (30%)."[7]

Another concern my wife and I often hear from other parents is how their kids use screens as a means of escape. Virtual reality feels like the new actuality for Gen Z. They're not physically visiting places. They merely view them online from the comfort of their own homes. Gen Z seems okay with exchanging physical experiences for artificial ones. And while they may have lots of selfies to indicate they were "in the moment," that doesn't mean they truly lived it.

A Restructured Brain

In 2016, the UK affiliate of Youth for Christ published their findings from a survey of a thousand eleven- to eighteen-year-olds. Here's what they learned about the main activities Gen Z does during their free time (participants could choose multiple responses):[8]

Watching YouTube videos	81%
Watching TV/films	77%
Using social media	74%
Spending time with friends	73%
Gaming	61%

It comes as no surprise that whether it's watching videos or engaging with social media, most Gen Zers spend more time on their phones than doing anything else. But what really stood out to me was that when asked what their top negative influences were, 67 percent of Gen Zers answered "social media," 41 percent said "friends," and 40 percent said "YouTubers."

Did you catch that? Although Gen Z admits that social media consumption is harmful, they still willingly spend most of their free time watching YouTube videos and viewing content on social media as their entertainment of choice.

The entertainment world is very effective at instilling values in our children that are antithetical to the Bible. As conservative commentator Matt Walsh points out:

Americans spend about eleven hours a day consuming media in various forms. This would be a problem irrespective of faith, because it prevents us from living an authentic human existence and reduces us to the status of spectators. But the problem is exacerbated for Christians because much of the media we ingest is avowedly hostile to Christianity.[9]

I can't tell you how many students I've spoken with on campuses and in churches who tell me how they came across a podcast or YouTube channel claiming to "expose" the lies of Christianity (or words to that effect).

Another strange and relatively new phenomenon that scientists and doctors are observing in younger patients is "tech neck." It's a condition caused by looking down at phones for long periods of time. Researchers have also noted atypical bone growth in some young people, which they attribute to bad posture due to excessive screen time.[10]

And that's not all. The effects of screen time are far more wide-ranging than a restructuring of the brain and body. According to the American Academy of Pediatrics (AAP), parents should limit how much time their children spend on devices every day because research shows that kids who have no restrictions or oversight regarding screen time can experience more stress and depression, have trouble sleeping, and struggle with eating disorders.[11]

Other studies reveal that high levels of screen time can contribute to memory problems for children[12] and indeed cause unhappiness.[13]

Beyond Stressed Out

You might think that having the latest phone and connecting more easily with friends on Snapchat would enhance your Gen Z kid's social life, yet it's actually having the opposite effect. Go figure.

According to *The Economist*, "Generation Z is stressed, depressed, and exam-obsessed."[14] That pretty much summarizes the mental state of Gen Z. Current research also tells us that older Gen Zers in high school and entering college are considered the most stressed group in America.[15] Another report states that younger teens who consume social media throughout the day report being more depressed than older teens.[16]

One high school student recently told me, "It doesn't matter what I do. . . . I can pray, try talking to my parents, or keep distracted by texting, but the anxiety that I feel never seems to go away." And when I asked an eighth grader how she felt after scrolling through her friends' pics on Instagram, her answer was not surprising: "I sometimes feel added pressure to try to be someone who matches what I see from everybody else."

It's not easy for Gen Zers entering adolescence to handle the emotional pressures that come with comparing themselves to everyone else. The psychological stress young people experience is also potentially harmful to young, developing brains. Replacing human interaction with constant screen time can negatively affect a child's cognitive abilities and impede interpersonal interactions.

IF YOU'RE FEELING ANXIOUS, WHAT MAKES YOU FEEL BETTER? [17]			
Listening to music	26%	Being on social media	
Talking with someone	24%	platforms	3%
Watching videos/movies/TV	14%	Interacting with animals	3%
Meditating	11%	Reading	3%
Sleeping	9%	Praying/reading the Bible	2%
Gaming	9%	Using drugs/alcohol	2%
Doing physical activity	7%	Doing art	1%
Eating food	5%	Journaling or writing	1%
Spending time in solitude	4%	*Other*	8%

Stress-inducing situations can make or break your child's confidence and ability to resolve conflict. A troubling trend among millions of Gen Zers is that they get so caught up in studying for the test that they fail to understand not only the material but also the process of learning.[18] It makes you wonder, *What exactly is my Gen Z kid learning after all is said and done?*

We've seen the correlation between screens and stress, but another significant link we can't ignore is the de-motivation caused in the brain. Think about it—the stimuli of high-tech culture connecting to high-speed service is causing Gen Z to rely on instant convenience and satisfaction. I've been around hundreds, if not thousands, of Gen Zers, and one thing is for sure: They are an impatient generation that often lacks the skill and motivation to overcome adversity.

Trouble Sleeping

Along with stress and de-motivation, another common side effect of too much screen time is sleep deprivation. Gen Zers, on average, get nearly two hours less sleep a night than recommended by experts, a figure largely attributable to increased use among younger generations of sleep-disruptive technologies such as video games, computers, and smartphones.[19]

It's not only the amount of time Gen Z spends on their smartphones that is an issue but also *when* they're looking at them. After speaking at a high school graduation, I asked the students if they checked their phones either right before bed or while lying in bed. Out of the approximately fifty graduates, only three of them said no.

This is a particular problem among Gen Zers because the screens on these devices essentially trick the brain into thinking it is still daylight. The blue light from the devices inhibits the body's production of melatonin—a hormone released by the pineal gland to help the body fall asleep. (Using "dark mode" on a device might reduce the amount of blue light stimulating the brain, but it's not enough.)

Aside from blue light, when your son or daughter is lying in bed and receives a text or hears that telltale alert coming from their phone, their brain produces dopamine—a chemical that makes them perk up. That's the last thing their body should be producing while trying to fall asleep. Either way, constantly checking one's phone before bed or during the night is a common cause of sleep deprivation—for parents and children alike.

Exposed to Porn

Another consequence of Gen Z's preoccupation with technology is easy exposure to pornography. The average age of exposure to Internet porn has been dropping for years; the average age is thirteen, though some children are exposed as early as five.[20] There's also the frequent sharing of nude photos among teens—what kids these days call "noodz." One of the most disturbing things for any parent to learn is that their child has been sexting. I remember hearing from a couple who just found out that their daughter had sent nude pics to her boyfriend. Even worse, the boy had been sharing the "noodz" with his friends.

Another student, a nineteen-year-old named Dustyn, told me that he viewed porn virtually every day. I asked if his parents were aware of his porn struggle. Dustyn acknowledged that they were and had even taken the extra step of installing filtering software on his devices.

"Has that helped?" I asked. The look on his face told me that it hadn't. Dustyn confessed that he'd found work-arounds so he could still look at porn.

This, dear parents, is exactly what Satan wants. Modern technology has enabled systems that offer both incessant entertainment and explicit porn. It exploits our children beginning at an early age and often leads to full-fledged addiction while they are still teenagers.

Overweight and Overmedicated

Ask yourself a question: If Gen Z children's number one activity is spending hours on their devices, how much physical exercise are they getting? The answer: probably not much.

At a summer youth event, I asked the audience of students to describe their generation. A nineteen-year-old responded, "Gen Z is lazy, easily offended, and biblically illiterate." A sixteen-year-old got up from her chair and voiced her concerns about her and her friends' struggles with weight and poor eating habits.

But that's a prevailing storyline with Gen Z: Too much technology affects a child's mood and behavioral patterns, increases aggression and anxiety, and can lead to heart disease and obesity.

The Centers for Disease Control and Prevention reports that of the six million children who have been diagnosed with attention deficit hyperactivity disorder (ADHD), nearly 70 percent of six- to seventeen-year-olds are treated with medication.[21] I've seen for myself that Gen Z's dependence on ADHD meds has become a serious problem in high schools and on college campuses.

All across our university campuses, students flock to get their hands on Adderall, or "Addy" for short. "I'm addicted to 'Addy,'" one student told me. "I need it to stay focused and do my homework." Over time, however, students become immune to a certain level of Adderall. Whereas twenty milligrams used to do the trick, now that's no longer enough. So students start experimenting by mixing their prescription drugs with other substances to create a sustained stimulus. This increases the risk of an accidental overdose. And for what—to stay awake studying late into the night? Not worth it.

The "Madderall" craze speaks to the anxiety, worry, and angst that Gen Zers cope with while dealing with the pressure of achieving good grades. A team from *The Economist* reported that for most young students, getting good grades was a bigger worry than getting caught drinking or dealing with an unplanned pregnancy.[22]

— — —

These expectations don't always originate from the students. Much of the "pressure for perfectionism" among high school and college students is brought on by their parents.[23] Unrealistic expectations can cause children to think less of themselves and feel overwhelmed. And many of these students, in trying to manage parental expectations and added stress, turn to drugs and alcohol to help them study or simply cope with the pressure.[24]

The statistics and symptoms that result from our kids' digital obsessions are not merely alarming—they're frightening! But sometimes—especially when it comes to the dangers of device addiction—we need to be reminded of and confronted with the facts, no matter how unpleasant. For example, in his book *Parenting Generation Screen: Guiding Your Kids to Be Wise in a Digital World*, author Jonathan McKee puts it simply: "Pedophiles have existed for millennia, but now they have unrestricted access to kids who are sharing way too much about themselves and are desperate for 'followers.'"[25]

Additionally, the nonprofit organization Partnership to End Addiction conveys this strongly worded warning: "Parents are not effectively communicating the dangers of Rx medicine misuse and abuse to their kids, nor are they safeguarding their medications at home and disposing of unused medications properly."[26]

STRATEGIES TO BRING FREEDOM

By now you're probably feeling overwhelmed as a parent! But it is still possible to communicate with your kids about these dangers and implement strategies that can go a long way toward freeing them from obsessive habits with their devices. That's why the rest of this chapter is devoted to teaching you how to put into practice a few valuable tips.

But before we begin, I don't want to leave you with the impression that every single Gen Zer is an overweight, depressed, screen-addicted slacker who aimlessly goes through life with no good path to adulthood. That's not true. I'm sure you know of several Gen Zers, as I do, who've set limits on their device usage and have developed good communication skills. Perhaps some of them are your children. Either way, I hope you find some benefit from the following strategies.

The First Strategy: Speak Their Language

After discussing with a middle-aged couple the importance of regular conversations with their teens, they both looked at me with blank stares.

"Does that not make sense to the two of you?" I asked with a concerned expression.

The dad looked over at his wife and then back at me. He nervously rubbed his hands together. "This may sound like we're horrible parents," he said, "considering we've now been parents for over twenty years—"

"Doug," I interjected, "you know I don't see you and Martha like that. You two are great parents. Just say what needs to be said."

"Go on, honey," Martha encouraged her husband.

"All right," Doug began. "Well, it's just, um . . . it's just that Martha and I don't do a very good job talking to our kids. I'll give you an example: One time I knocked on my daughter's door to check on her after I came home from work. She never even turned around from her desk to acknowledge me. It was like I wasn't even there."

"That's just one example," added Martha. "There are plenty of instances when Doug or I try to talk to our kids, but they never really respond. As a mother—and this is very unpleasant for me to say—I almost feel like they don't like us."

As you probably know, an essential part of good communication is understanding the other person, and every generation has its own way of speaking. I don't know about your era, but for me, growing up in the 1980s, we said things like "That's rad!" "Duh!" "Take a chill pill!" and "Psych!" The meanings were pretty straightforward, at least to us. But Gen Z are digital natives with a language all their own. Trendy words and phrases come and go as they continuously invent new slang. For example, the following terms were popular among Gen Z when I was writing this book, but some might already be obsolete by the time you're reading it:

1. *Extra*—dramatic or over the top
2. *Big yikes*—an exclamation used when someone is super embarrassed
3. *Ghost*—to ignore someone completely, especially when texting
4. *Go off*—encouraging someone to keep talking because you like what they're saying; also a sarcastic response when you disagree
5. *Fam*—one's closest friends who are not biological family members
6. *Flex*—to show off or brag
7. *Salty*—acting jealous, annoyed, or upset
8. *Snack*—an attractive person

9. *Sip tea*—to listen to other people gossip
10. *Vibe check*—asking friends how they're feeling; also said as a warning before punching someone

Did you notice that some of these terms have multiple meanings—some of which are virtually the opposite of the first meaning? The point is that parents should attempt to stay in the know by keeping up with Gen Z slang, just so they can understand what Gen Z is talking about! (And yes, you can certainly "flex" a little right now if you already knew some of these terms.)

I'm not sure of the original source—or even if it's real—but I thought you might get a kick out of this text exchange between a mom and her son. It shows what can happen when parents misinterpret texting slang.

The Second Strategy: Engage in Daily, Face-to-Face Conversations
Isn't it interesting that young people who spend the most time on their devices are often the ones who complain the most about being lonely? Since the first days of the pandemic quarantine, millions

of people have taken to video platforms like Zoom, Google Meet, Microsoft Teams, and others to stay connected.

We have already examined how much time the average Gen Zers spend on their screens. If they're not texting, they're gaming. If they're not gaming, they're streaming or binge-watching. If they're not streaming, they're on TikTok or Snapchat or Instagram. (Facebook is so "over" among Gen Z.) Spending so much time in front of screens can not only alter the mood of our kids but also cause them to shut others out—particularly family members. Bear in mind that Gen Z isn't streaming simply to be entertained. Screens are also a means of escape—from loneliness, stress, and depression.

That's why one of the best remedies is more face-to-face conversations with parents and other adults. The more you incorporate this simple—and, shall I say, *humanistic*—interaction with your kids, the less dependent they will be on their screens.

One of the standards that legendary basketball coach Mike Krzyzewski (or "Coach K") implemented for the US Olympic team in 2012 was that everybody needed to demonstrate eye-to-eye contact when speaking to one another. This was a team showcasing all-time greats like LeBron James, Kobe Bryant, and Kevin Durant. Yet despite the larger-than-life talent on the roster, Coach K still insisted that his players look at each other when communicating.

That's what we as parents need to get back to. We need to sit down with our kids and have regular, meaningful conversations with them—on a daily basis if possible. By promoting healthy dialogue with your kids, you teach them how to express their concerns, work out problems, and even enjoy each other's company.

The Third Strategy: Show Interest in What Interests Them
Make a habit of letting your kids pick topics of conversation that interest them. If and when your Gen Z child brings up a particular

subject, be sure to pay attention and remain sensitive to how they *feel* about the issue rather than turn it into an argument.

When you interject your own opinion or overreact about how your son or daughter views a specific topic, it will only create more friction and inhibit future conversations. First Peter 3:9-11 reads, "Do not repay evil for evil or reviling for reviling, but on the contrary, bless, for to this you were called, that you may obtain a blessing. For 'Whoever desires to love life and see good days, let him keep his tongue from evil and his lips from speaking deceit; let him turn away from evil and do good; let him seek peace and pursue it.'"

Peter encourages Christians to refrain from insulting or speaking evil about someone, even if that person shows evil intent. As a Christian parent, you need to set the example for your children by speaking well of others—including your children—and maintaining unity and peace.

The Fourth Strategy: Hear Them Out

When communicating face-to-face with your kids, be sure to welcome their individuality and pay attention to their emotional outlook on life. I like to think of the iconic voice of R&B artist Charles Wright singing his 1970 hit song "Express Yourself." That's what you need to help your children do. Let your kids speak their minds and express how they are feeling. Exactly what this looks like will vary depending on the age, gender, and maturity of each child.

Some good advice on this comes from the book *You Just Don't Understand* by Deborah Tannen. Tannen describes many of the differences in the ways that boys and girls communicate. When girls talk, Tannen says, they seek to connect, touch, and build rapport. Boys, meanwhile, communicate to establish their social position and like to exchange information.[27] Keep this in mind when engaging with your own son or daughter.

Some conversations will stem from those random times when you come to your children's rooms to check on them or ask how their day went. Other, more intentional, conversations will require you to be sensitive to their mood swings and invite them to share what's on their minds.

I was speaking at a parenting conference when a friend shared that he gives his kids the freedom to choose the time and place when they want to speak their minds. I've since put that advice into practice with my own kids. But I do have a confession: There have been times (not *that* many, I hope!) when I've influenced my kids' decisions to talk things out by suggesting (please don't judge me) a visit to the nearest Dairy Queen.

Here are a few sample statements that might help you communicate more effectively with your child:

- "I understand that you are upset, but let's find a better way to communicate how you feel."
- "Let's find a way to resolve this together."
- "Do you think getting angry is going to help you get what you want?"
- "I wanted to have some time with just the two of us because I can tell that something is bothering you."

WHAT *IS* THE RIGHT SMARTPHONE AGE?

Did you really think I would end this chapter without addressing the big question on many parents' minds?

At what age should I let my kids have a smartphone or other device?

After all, we have age restrictions for many other freedoms

and responsibilities. You have to be sixteen years old to drive, eighteen to vote and serve in the military, and twenty-one to buy alcohol. But at what age should parents hand over a phone to their kids?

Is there some magic age that makes it okay?

I've found that parents give their kids devices at all ages. For example, I once met a middle-aged mother, Susan, who let me know she had read my book *Abandoned Faith* about how many millennials today are forsaking the faith of their youth.

"I do have a question," Susan said, "if you don't mind . . ."

"I don't mind!" I said with enthusiasm. "I love questions. Fire away."

Susan was clearly relieved. "Before asking you what my husband and I should do, let me explain the situation," she began. "Last Christmas we decided to give our daughter and son phones. We are now regretting that decision. They are constantly on their phones, and my son recently downloaded some games and additional app content that cost over a hundred dollars."

At this point, Susan stopped talking and looked away for a moment to regain her composure.

"Sorry about that," she resumed. "I'm just still a little frustrated by all this. So my question is, what should we do now with our kids' phones? Should we take them away?"

"How old were your kids when you gave them phones for Christmas?" I asked.

"My daughter was thirteen, and my son was ten at the time."

I'll get back to Susan's story in a moment. But before I do, let me also tell you about Eric's situation.

After church one Sunday, Eric and I walked out of the building together. He told me that he was tired of arguing with his son over the amount of time he spent looking at screens. I asked Eric, "How much time does your son spend on his devices?"

Eric struggled to answer the question, so I followed up by asking, "Do you know what he's doing on his devices?"

"To be honest with you, no, not really," he replied.

Stories like Susan's and Eric's are typical of what I've encountered with many parents. They are confused about when to give a phone to their child, and then they often struggle to keep up with how their child is using the device.

— — —

I want to pause for a moment and have you take a quiz. Don't be alarmed—this brief series of questions is meant to help you be more aware and proactive regarding screens and your kids.

1. At what age did you give your kids a smartphone or other mobile device?
2. What's the average amount of time your kids spend on their screens every day?
3. Do you know who they're texting and what they're viewing?
4. Do you know what apps they like to use? Did you approve these apps?
5. Do you know whether your kids have been exposed to porn?
6. Have you placed any restrictions on their screen usage? Have you installed any content filters or made use of any parental controls on their phones?

I don't know how you responded to the quiz, but you do. Perhaps you were pleased with your answers; maybe you were disappointed. Either way, it does little good to fret about the past. But you *can* be more proactive moving forward.

— — —

Now let's get back to Susan and Eric.

List some mistakes you think Susan and her husband made with their kids.

_____

_____

List some mistakes you think Eric made with his son.

_____

_____

I want to be clear: This exercise isn't about bashing Susan and Eric. The purpose is to learn from their experiences. Susan and Eric aren't bad parents; they just both made particular (some would say questionable) decisions and are now regretting them.

With that in mind, let's walk through some constructive steps that will safeguard your child, set appropriate boundaries, and give you the control you want *and* need as a parent when it comes to devices in the home.

1. *Think twice before giving preteens their own smartphones.* This doesn't mean that your children can never use a device to help with their homework, watch a movie, or play a game. But in my opinion, it's neither wise nor healthy for younger kids to have access to an Internet-accessing device they can take with them wherever they go.

   The moment you say to your twelve-year-old, "Here you go! Your father and I got you your own smartphone [or iPad, or whatever]," not only will they become quite possessive of it, but it will likely also become a point of contention. Plus, think about what you're handing them. You're not just allowing them to text their friends or play some games; you're handing them a powerful computer that gives them almost unlimited access to the digital world.

I've already addressed the potential damage and dangers associated with spending too much time on devices, especially for children. With that in mind, do you know how old someone needs to be to sign up for any of the top social media platforms? Thirteen. That's largely due to 1998 federal legislation called the Children's Online Privacy Protection Act, which restricts websites from tracking data of anyone under thirteen. (Even Congress recognized the need to protect young children online.) That's why I probably wouldn't consider entrusting your child with a device until he or she is at least thirteen or fourteen years old.

Keep in mind that you know your children better than I do, and that this age range might not be best for your kids. All children are not the same. Boys and girls are not the same. Maybe some of your kids need to mature a bit more before you hand them their own screens. In fact, I've talked with several teens who told me they didn't get their first phone until they were fifteen or sixteen.

I believe that many parents (myself included) need to take a hard look at the amount of "parent pressure" we succumb to. Parent pressure is exactly what it sounds like— peer pressure for parents. In other words, if all the other parents let their ten-year-olds have phones, then who are you to be the only holdout?

What is our duty as parents? Are we supposed to make decisions regarding our kids based on the pressures of the culture around us, or should we make those decisions based on our faith and our convictions? As parents, as leaders, we are not to give in to the pressures of the world at large. We don't surrender our responsibility simply to avoid being the "strict parent"; nor do we give in to our kids' demands just because their friends have phones and they don't.

2. Before granting your child access to a screen and all the social media that comes with it, *make sure that you (and your spouse, if you're married) sit down with your children to discuss specific guidelines and expectations.* If your kids don't agree to your terms, then I suggest that they not have a device. Your job is to hold them accountable for what they view, post, and share. I've known some parents who drafted a "contract" for smartphone use and required their kids to sign it.

3. *Monitor the amount of time your kids spend on their screens and be aware of how they're using them.* I can't stress this enough: Setting boundaries is only half the process—you have to enforce them! Many parents establish guidelines with their kids yet fail to monitor their actual usage and activity. That's not fair to your kids. They might not like you checking their phone or making sure that the parental controls are working properly, but you don't need to feel bad—you're just doing your job as a parent. You're protecting them from potential danger, and you're holding them accountable to abide by the rules you all agreed to.

4. *Be sure to enforce consequences if your children go behind your back and violate the guidelines you've established.* I encourage parents to come up with some consequences beforehand—ones that you will follow through on. I suggest practical ones; for example, if your child doesn't act responsibly with a smartphone, then perhaps that child shouldn't have one for a while. (I'll talk more about implementing consequences in chapter 9.)

5. *Make use of any available parental controls; install filtering software for your home Internet service and on your children's devices.* I like to save money as much as the next guy, but this is not the time to cut corners. We have no problem spending money on locks for our doors and even home security systems, so spending a few dollars a month on our kids' well-being while they are on their devices shouldn't be an issue. In my experience, you can find good parental control software for an annual cost of less than a hundred dollars. (My wife and I have used a product called Qustodio for several years to manage our family's mobile devices, and we also take advantage of the parental controls on our Internet router at home.)

6. *Have ongoing conversations with your kids about the good and bad of technology*—and ask them if they've come across anything online that's bothered them or made them feel uncomfortable. Since our two older children have recently enrolled in college classes, my wife and I have been very cautious regarding just how much personal information they make public online. Just the other day, one of my boys showed me a random text he received inviting him to click a link to have sex with people in the area.

   Troubling, right? My friends, this happens all the time. If you have access to Netflix, I encourage you to watch a documentary called *The Social Dilemma*. I watched it with my kids. The documentary features a host of tech veterans who spent time at Google, Facebook, YouTube, and other digital giants. Some of these experts helped develop the technology that these companies operate. They know the secret sauce, and they reveal how Big Tech is spying on us—feeding us inaccurate or unwanted information, analyzing our search patterns and selling the data, plus sending us unsolicited notifications in an effort to keep us on our devices (and their platforms in particular) for ever-longer periods of time. So stay alert, be informed, and pray faithfully that your children can stand strong against the schemes and temptations that plague the digital realm.

I want to acknowledge that my wife and I didn't do the best job with our two oldest when we gave them their first screens. Sure, we did a few of the six steps listed above, but our guidelines weren't very clear, and we came up with consequences on the fly. I share this with you because these steps didn't suddenly come to us the moment we brought Tyler home from the hospital. No, I developed them through much trial and error. So don't feel bad if you've made mistakes. We all do. Instead, make a commitment now to review these six steps and to learn from past mistakes.

Parenting Practice

1. Before placing limits on your kids' devices, try setting a good example for them. If you're always on your phone, watching TV, or browsing on your iPad, how do you think your kids are going to behave with their devices?

2. Find ways to reduce the amount of time each day that your family spends on screens, including TV and video games. Whatever limits you settle on, whether it's thirty minutes a day or three hours, be sure to remain consistent.

3. Establish reasonable restrictions. Here are some that we've implemented in our home: (1) no computers, tablets, or TVs in our kids' bedrooms, (2) no devices during dinner or while doing homework, and (3) time limits on gaming and screen time each day.

4. Enforce age restrictions for different technologies/apps in your home, and make sure each device complies with your desired privacy settings.

5. Teach your kids (and model for them) to not take their phones to bed with them.

6. Consider setting aside Sundays as a day to "fast" from tech and a chance to "reset" for the week ahead.

7. Look for ways to use technology as another tool for teaching your kids. Whether it's streaming a positive movie, watching an instructional YouTube video, or using an interactive app, screens offer many opportunities to teach your children about faith and worldview issues.

8. Make time to catch up with your children each week to see how they are doing with life, family, and faith. Reinforce your commitment to always be there for them, and demonstrate how much you love spending time with them.

9. Finally, here are some tips to help your children deal with stress in their lives: (1) Pray with them regularly. (2) Help them figure out what sorts of situations cause them to be anxious. (3) Put together a plan to help them respond to stress. (4) Together, find specific Bible verses to help combat their anxiety. (5) Assist them in reorganizing their schedules so they have time to rest and spend time in contemplation. (6) If stress and anxiety remain issues, be open to the idea that your child might benefit from seeing a licensed Christian counselor.

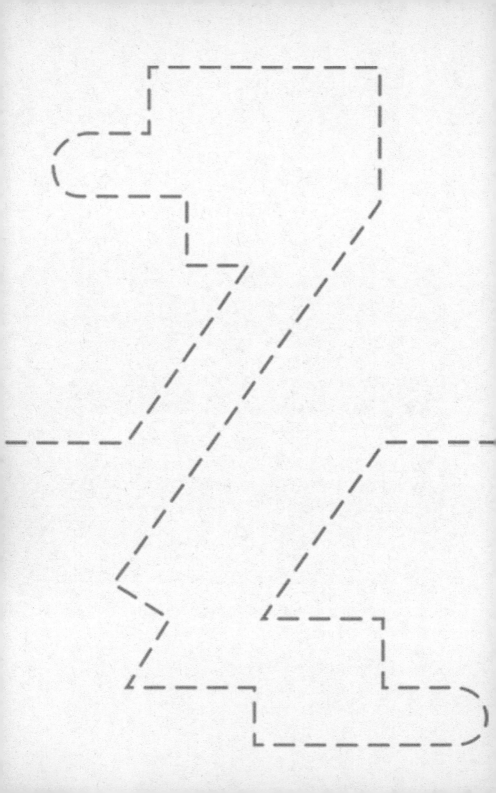

5

DEPLETED FAITH

MORE THAN HALF OF GEN ZERS reject Christianity,[1] and many see it as an intolerant or hypocritical religion that is both out of touch with society and out of step with the culture.[2] So how can parents combat the false worldviews shaping Gen Z? Let me share a conversation I had with a parent going through this very thing.

"How did your talk with Nathan go?" I asked Jon, a father of three.

Jon was visibly apprehensive about sharing with me what he and his son had discussed.

"Jon," I said, "if you feel your conversation with Nathan is private, then by all means keep it between the two of you."

Jon quickly reassured me that he didn't mind sharing what his son had said. The problem he was having was that he didn't know where to start when describing their relationship.

"Nathan grew up in the church," Jon finally began. "His

mother and I divorced when he was nine," he continued. "She soon remarried, and not long after that I met Jennifer. I'll admit that I wasn't really there for my son after the divorce. I was in a very bad place at the time. When things got better, I would get him every other weekend. He loves baseball, so we'd go out to eat and catch a ball game. Sometimes in the car ride home or when I'd be taking him to school, Nathan would ask me some pretty tough questions, like 'Why did you and Mom divorce?' and 'If God is real, why doesn't He do something about all the evil in the world?'"

"Wow," I interjected. "Nathan seems like quite the philosopher. Has he always asked these sorts of deep questions?"

"I guess so," Jon replied, a bit of regret in his tone. "To tell you the truth, when I look back, I didn't pay much attention to his questions or what was going on in his heart when he was younger."

"And now?" I asked Jon. I was curious to find out what had transpired with Nathan.

But Jon didn't answer. He just sat there, his arms folded and his head down.

"Jon?" I said. "Look at me. Please."

Jon slowly raised his head, took a glance around the room, and then settled his eyes on me.

"Did your conversation with your son have anything to do with him telling you he no longer believes in Christianity?" I asked.

"Yes," Jon said. "Nathan pretty much told his mother and me that he's now an atheist."

Jon's story isn't that unusual these days. I was recently part of a Zoom meeting with a Christian school, and many faculty members mentioned how "unchristian" many of their students are. The principal went so far as to say that a growing number of students refuse to attend chapel services.

A few months back, I received an email from a mother who

had read my book *Abandoned Faith*. This mother wrote to express her concerns for her two daughters, who were apparently making poor choices. She said both girls grew up in a Christian home but had stopped attending church and started drinking after entering college.

"It makes me so sad and disappointed that they do not want to follow God's plans," wrote this desperate parent. "And yet our daughters still expect us to financially support them and put up with their rude behavior when they come home to visit. *What should my husband and I do?*"

I wish I could tell you this sort of situation is uncommon. But in my experience, it's not. Whether I'm teaching about worldview at Summit Ministries, working with Focus on the Family, or speaking at a church conference, I meet countless parents who tell me about their Gen Z children who have abandoned the Christian faith. I even have students come up to me after speaking engagements *at church* and object to my claims about Christianity. I don't mind responding to people's objections to my faith. That's not the problem. My concern is the increasing frequency of such challenges, especially in church.

But why? Why are so many Gen Zers, raised in the church and in the faith, now deconverting from Christianity?

4 PERCENT

In March 2020, the world went into quarantine. The COVID-19 virus acted as an invader. When it entered a person's system, it attacked healthy cells by latching on and duplicating itself to the point that the body couldn't fight off the virus. A few days after exposure, the infected person often showed flu-like symptoms that could even lead to death.

The coronavirus was such an enormous threat because it essentially came out of nowhere. Experts from around the world raced to create a vaccine.

But our kids today face even more dangerous threats: competing worldviews that confuse their minds and hearts. Author and pastor Paul David Tripp puts it like this: "There *is* a battle raging in the lives of young people, but it is not the battle of biology. It is an intensely spiritual battle, a battle for the heart."[3]

Indeed, Gen Z is locked in intense spiritual warfare over their souls.

We've danced to this song before regarding the millennial generation. For years, we've been inundated with statistics showing how unchristian millennials are. So when I say that Gen Z is remaking America into a post-Christian nation, it might sound like old news. But I am telling you now, Mom and Dad, that the generation you are currently raising is made up of more non-Christians than any previous group (and that's including millennials).

America, once a nation made up primarily of Christians, now contains *two* generations that largely reject Christianity.

Of the Gen Zers who do identify as Christian, just 4 percent of them have a solid understanding of the Bible. The Barna Group and Impact 360 Institute uncovered this truth in their published research about Gen Z. Their report states, "Many in Generation Z, more than in generations before them, are a spiritual blank slate. They are drawn to things spiritual, but their starting point is vastly different from previous generations, many of whom received a basic education on the Bible and Christianity. The worldview of Gen Z, by contrast, is truly post-Christian. They were not born into a Christian culture, and it shows."[4]

Since my early days working first with millennials, and now with Gen Z, I've seen firsthand the drift away from biblical truth as society moves from one generation to the next.

Both millennials and Gen Zers have undergone a large-scale deconstruction of their faith. In my past ten years of teaching apologetics full-time to young people, a reoccurring theme among Gen Z is increased questioning—and rejecting—what they've been taught about God, the Bible, and the truth claims of Christianity. Parents tell me that their Gen Z children are dispassionate about attending church and disinterested in reading the Bible. In an alarming 2018 article titled "Atheism Doubles Among Generation Z," the Barna Group reported that more than half of Gen Zers said church is either "not too" (27 percent) or "not at all" (27 percent) important. More to the point, 46 percent of self-identified Gen Z Christians agreed that "church is not relevant to me personally."[5]

Recent General Social Survey data from thirty-five thousand Americans indicates that religious "nones" now encompass about 23 percent of America's adults. This means that nearly one out of every four adults in the United States, when asked about their religious identity, say "none." Further, many who were once part of the church are now leaving it.

James Emery White, in his book *Meet Generation Z*, clears up some confusion about what the term *nones* actually means among members of Gen Z. "The real mark of the nones," he writes, "is not a rejection of God but a rejection of any specific religion. When it comes to content, dogma, orthodoxy—anything spelled out or offering a system of beliefs—they've gone from 'I believe' to 'Maybe' to 'Who knows?' When pressed as to what they do hold to, they collectively answer, 'Nothing in particular.'"[6]

— — —

A few months back, I was talking to some high school and college students at a Christian camp in Maryland. I bluntly asked the group how many of them genuinely wanted to be there. Two of the nine students raised their hands. Noticing they were outnumbered, the two students quickly lowered their hands.

I wasn't surprised, but I did want to know why the other seven didn't want to be at the camp. After all, I was the speaker at the camp, and I kind of felt like a loser knowing that these students didn't want to be there.

"Why did only two students raise their hands?" I asked.

For the next thirty minutes or so, the other seven students candidly shared how faith in God made little or no sense to them. One student challenged me, "If God exists, why is there evil and suffering in the world?" Another student said, "I can't stand organized religion and the negative connotations associated with it." That particular comment prompted one girl, Jamie, to let the group know that when she identified as gay, her church back home told her she couldn't come back.

"My parents forced me to come to this camp, hoping that I'll find Jesus or something," she told the group. "I think they're going to be sorely disappointed when I go back home and I'm still gay."

I don't know what happened to those nine students after they left camp, but I continue to hear from many millennials and Gen Zers why they don't attend church anymore or why they've decided to deconvert from Christianity. To be clear, however, they are not actually *leaving* Christianity.

What do I mean by that?

What I mean is that even when you combine millennials and Gen Zers, fewer than 15 percent are biblically literate. This tells us that more than 80 percent of these two generations were already biblically illiterate (they don't know much about Christianity and the Bible) and that a large number of them thought they were Christians but actually were not. In other words, many millennials and Gen Zers haven't been taught a biblical version of Christianity.

Instead, they've experienced (for the most part) a watered-down or culturally acceptable version of Christianity. I'm talking about *maybe* an hour of church a week, combined with little to no Bible reading or instruction through the week and close to zero doctrinal training.

In his classic book *The Cost of Discipleship*, the German pastor and theologian Dietrich Bonhoeffer compares two types of "grace" that, in effect, produced two different kinds of Christians in Germany during the rise and reign of Adolf Hitler. In one camp, Bonhoeffer writes, is "cheap grace"—a grace without discipleship and without the Cross of Jesus Christ. Bonhoeffer describes how cheap grace cares only about the benefits that come with Christianity, ignoring the call to commit to its truths and to live a life of sacrifice.[7]

In the other camp, Bonhoeffer writes, is "costly grace":

> Such grace is costly because it calls us to follow, and it is
> grace because it calls us to follow Jesus Christ. It is costly
> because it costs a man his life, and it is grace because it gives
> a man the only true life. It is costly because it condemns sin,
> and grace because it justifies the sinner. Above all, it is costly
> because it cost God the life of his Son.[8]

I bring up Bonhoeffer's two types of grace because they speak to the cheapened version of Christianity that characterizes much of Gen Z's faith—or lack thereof.

Many Gen Zers grew up believing that all they needed to do was raise their hand to receive Jesus in their heart. Just repeat the prayer with that person up front at church, and that's it—you're good to go! But after this "conversion," there's no plan of action, no follow-up, no discipleship, and certainly no Bible training and instruction in the fundamentals of Christianity. I've seen countless young people accept Jesus as little more than a "burden remover" and then continue their lives with little in the way of spiritual transformation. Want to hold to viewpoints contrary to the Bible? No problem. Yet if you were to ask them, most would say that they are definitely Christians.

For the sake of clarity, I'm not knocking altar calls at church or disqualifying salvations that resulted from raising a hand or praying a prayer. What I'm pointing out is that this initial *profession* of faith is not the end of the believer's journey—it's just the beginning. In the Bible, we see many passages about professing faith (John 1:12; Acts 16:31; Romans 10:9-10; Ephesians 2:8-9; 1 Peter 1:21), but we see even more in the Bible about the *progression* of faith (Psalm 119; 1 Corinthians 15:58; Galatians 5:16-24; Ephesians 4:11-16; 5:15-17; 6:10-18; Philippians 1:9; 3:10; Colossians 1:9-12; 2 Timothy 2:15; James 1:22-27; 2 Peter 1:5-8).

(Personally, I have a problem with churches that push professions of faith for younger children and teens yet offer very little guidance when it comes to the progression of that faith.)

So where does this leave Gen Z? It leaves them believing and living out a partial gospel that has produced a generation with a fragmented faith. This, I believe, is part of the reason why so many of them have abandoned Christianity. As I mentioned earlier, most Gen Zers aren't dumping genuine, biblical Christianity. Sure, some are, but most deconversions involve younger adults leaving behind the cheap-grace form of Christianity, which is not a true picture of the gospel.

This trend is both good and bad. Here's the good news: Many Gen Zers recognize that if cheap-grace Christianity is what it's all about, they are not interested. Therefore, instead of turning away from a biblical or costly-grace Christianity, many in Gen Z are deconverting from a partial gospel—a watered-down version of Christianity.

But if millions of young people have already walked away, how do we tackle the task of bringing them back? Because the bad news is that deconverted Gen Zers now have a different response to Christianity: "Why would I go back to an oppressive religion that is anti-gay and didn't work for me in the first place?" Furthermore, how can we equip already-doubting Gen Zers with a more robust biblical worldview?

Before we throw up our hands in defeat, let's keep in mind that we serve the almighty God of the universe. Let's also take a closer look at what Gen Z believes about God, Jesus, and the Bible.

THE DECLINE OF CHRISTIAN TRUTH AMONG GEN Z

GOD TRUTH

Theism
63%

Atheism/
Agnosticism/
None
31%

Other
6%

Based on the sheer number of Gen Zers who claim to be atheists, at least a third of you reading this are probably raising a child who embraces atheism. Not only that, most of the 63 percent of Gen Zers who profess belief in God also say that the God of the Bible is the same as Allah in the Quran. Yet the God of Christianity is *not* the same as Allah of Islam.

As I discuss issues of faith with Gen Z, I've discovered that Gen Zers object to God's existence for four main reasons.

The first reason is the problem of evil and the presence of suffering in the world. Hundreds of Gen Zers claiming to be atheists have told me that they've never found a compelling argument for how God and evil can coexist. To them, if God exists, then God would eradicate evil. And since evil clearly exists, then God surely doesn't.

On my YouTube channel, I address this question in a video titled "Is God a Cruel Monster?" I can't count the number of comments I've received from young people blasting me for my perspective. Here are just two examples:

- "Yes. God is one of the most evil fictional characters ever created. God in the Old Testament is a monster! A bully! Because he is so powerful over his creations! Even until now. Look at this pandemic going on."

- "The fictional character of God in the Bible, as described in its historical fiction, is a monster. And so are you, trying to make up justifications for genocide. Shame on you."

It's not easy being on the receiving end of comments like these. But what bothers me most is the anger and confusion that many of these young people express.

The second reason is a sense that life has no purpose or meaning. This has become a disturbing trend among Gen Z. Because so many of them lack a feeling of purpose, Gen Zers are less likely to develop an interest in spiritual matters.

I've heard from many members of Gen Z who've watched some of my videos. The following email came from a nineteen-year-old who criticized me for claiming that Jesus offers us truth, meaning, and purpose:

Why do Christians like you feel you have a right to tell atheists like me that my life has purpose and meaning? It's nonsense to believe in a thing called "God," and it's absurd to think God came in human form and died a horrific death on the cross. Evolution teaches that we've evolved into human creatures without rhyme or reason. Therefore, life is without purpose.

Of course, not all Gen Z students think this way. Many others tell me that they don't really give much thought to God, evil, or whether they need faith in their lives. They just want to be left alone so they can live however they wish. They can do good in the world without God, they say. Instead, they would rather develop their own moral compass and establish a set of values and convictions based on their own perceptions.

But just because many Gen Zers reject religion, it doesn't necessarily mean they are not spiritual. A form of spirituality that some once labeled the New Age movement is trending again among young people. One student told me she dabbles in New Age practices because they calm her down when she's stressed. Another Gen Zer commented that New Age meditation helps bring balance to his life. I asked if he ever prays while meditating. "Sometimes," he said, then clarified that meditation isn't about talking to a deity as much as finding peace in the universe.

The third reason they often reject God's existence is the moral bankruptcy that Gen Z sees in their parents' generation. Gen Zers are so outraged by the hypocrisy and double standards of baby boomers, Generation X, and even some millennials that many young people have said, "Enough with Christianity." We already addressed some of these concerns in chapter 2 when looking at the four main parent groups currently raising Gen Z.

The fourth reason is the rejection or betrayal they've experienced in church. Gen Zers who deconvert from Christianity often cite intellectual reasons for their decision to leave the faith. And while this might be true, the emotional baggage they associate with church is also a major motivation for those decisions. Let me share an example of what this reasoning looks like.

— — —

Trad's dad was the pastor at his church. As Trad entered his tween years, he started to have severe doubts about his faith. One Sunday during a small-group session, Trad told his church friends that he'd recently concluded he was no longer a Christian. News of Trad's decision reached his dad rather quickly. Let's just say that things didn't go so well for Trad after that.

Several of Trad's friends stopped talking to him. Some parents in the church even told the youth pastor to make sure their children weren't around him—for fear that Trad might influence their kids to doubt their own Christian faith.

I grew angry as I listened to Trad recount his negative experience in his church. I could tell that he still hadn't gotten past the despair over how things had gone down with his church friends. His feelings of pain and rejection were still fresh.

Even though Trad had deconverted from Christianity, I thanked God that he still was drawn to attend a Christian conference where he made an effort to seek me out and share his story.

I hear these sorts of stories all the time. Speaking candidly, it's true that a lot of young people are being hurt by the church and that we need to do more to prevent these situations. That hurt or rejection leads many of them to feel bitter toward God and to lose out on experiencing community and a positive Christian influence in their lives. We need to help Gen Zers repair and rebuild their trust in the church and pick up the broken pieces of their faith.

But I don't want to place too much blame on the church, especially when much of what Gen Z hears and reads about Jesus Christ these days is false. Whether it comes from *New York Times* bestsellers like Bart Ehrman's *How Jesus Became God: The Exaltation of a Jewish Preacher from Galilee*, Reza Aslan's *Zealot: The Life and Times of Jesus of Nazareth*, and Dan Brown's *The Da Vinci Code*, or from countless schools and universities that seek to undermine the credibility of the Gospels—the story is much the same: There are very few outlets that Gen Z can turn to in order to find reliable and truthful information about Jesus.[9]

JESUS TRUTH

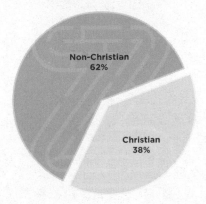

The pie chart above indicates that around 40 percent of Gen Z identify as Christians, yet very few Gen Zers feel confident enough to publicly express their personal faith in Christ.

Of all the generations in America today, Gen Z is the one most likely to believe that Jesus was only a man and certainly wasn't God. In some academic circles, there's a growing movement that suggests Jesus didn't even exist.

Gen Z is living in a time and place heavily influenced by YouTubers such as The Atheist Experience, The Thinking Atheist,

Cosmic Skeptic, and Paulogia. These channels (and lots of others) reduce Christianity to nothing more than a copycat religion, and they paint Jesus as a simple Jewish peasant who ruffled a few feathers back in the day and was eventually killed.

In the book *Gen Z: The Culture, Beliefs and Motivations Shaping the Next Generation*, the Barna Group (in partnership with Impact 360 Institute) expresses how insecure and confused members of Gen Z are when it comes to holding firm to what they believe:

> When it comes to statements of basic Christian orthodoxy,
> belief is not as strong in younger generations. Teens who
> believe in the historicity and divinity of Jesus, in his
> uniqueness as the only way to God and in the accuracy of
> the Bible's teachings are less likely than adults to say they
> are very convinced of their beliefs.[10]

Gen Z's growing uncertainty about Jesus is concerning. Later in this chapter, I'll offer a few suggestions regarding how to engage Gen Z about matters of faith. For now, however, I want you to have a better grasp of the current situation.

BIBLE TRUTH

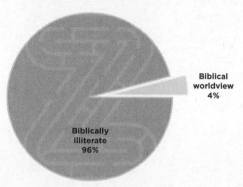

Biblical worldview 4%

Biblically illiterate 96%

There are two primary issues with Gen Z's attitude about the Bible. First, many Gen Zers deny the credibility of Scripture. Second, because they don't see the significance of the Bible for their everyday lives, many Gen Zers never pick it up and read it.

A friend of mine is a Bible teacher at a Christian high school. Several of his students have felt compelled to tell him that they believe the Bible is an ancient book with some value but not a divine book inspired by God.

One student in particular slammed a Bible against his desk and protested, "I am sick and tired of being told to believe the Bible. 'You need to trust in God's holy book,' my parents are always telling me. But does anyone ask me why I have problems with the Bible? Nope. And that's upsetting to me."

Silence filled the room. My buddy later told me he was so taken aback that he froze. He didn't know what to say.

Finally, a senior named Melanie broke the silence and said, "I think what we're trying to say is that we don't buy into Christianity because we're not convinced that the Bible is a reliable source."

For many Gen Zers, the Bible is for people who deny science and believe in legends. For example, only one in four Gen Zers believes science and the Bible are complementary.[11]

Gen Z is growing up in a culture largely hostile to Christianity— a culture where the public school system and university professors hold a naturalistic explanation of how humans came about. Students learn that science alone provides our knowledge of reality and that there is no purpose and meaning outside the natural universe. This explains the rise of atheism among Gen Z and why many in this current generation believe God and the Bible are not to be taken seriously. I'm reminded of a scene in the film *Nacho Libre* when the main character, Nacho, asks his sidekick, Esqueleto, why he hasn't been baptized. "I don't know why you always have to be judging me," Esqueleto responds, "because I only believe in *science*."

TALKING TO GEN Z ABOUT GOD, JESUS, AND THE BIBLE

Take a moment to consider your children. Do they think logically? How do they process and analyze information? Are they good at diagnosing problems and formulating solutions? Are they gullible, or do they ask probing questions to uncover the truth?

When I needed information as a child, I asked my mom to take me to the library. Once there, I had to use the Dewey decimal system to find the books I was looking for. This exercise was part of the learning process, and it helped me access the information and develop the skills I needed. The more I learned, the better able I was to articulate what I believed and why I believed it.

The rushed way that much of Gen Z retrieves information doesn't do much to advance their learning process. In fact, the ease with which they can access information is hindering Gen Z's ability to think for themselves. They are now accustomed to simply asking virtual assistants such as Siri or Alexa to tell them only what they want to know, and not a bit more. They have access to all the facts without any of the thoughts. As a result, many Gen Zers lack even the most basic critical thinking skills.

Without logical and critical thinking, how can we expect anyone to reach any well-reasoned conclusions about what is true or false, right or wrong, wise or foolish? Developing crucial reasoning skills can help safeguard your children by teaching them to sniff out unfounded claims and discern the truth more clearly.

Take photographs as an example. Anyone can take a picture with their phone. But to capture truly stunning photos requires a great deal of skill. The more you understand about adjusting settings like aperture, shutter speed, and ISO (the camera's sensitivity to light), the more likely you are to take sharper, more beautiful photos.

Similarly, for Gen Z to have a clearer outlook (or picture) of life, their views of God, Jesus, and the Bible need to be as sharp and clear as possible.

So when discussing these truths—the God of the Bible exists, Jesus is God in the flesh and the only way to God, and the Bible as the Word of God is trustworthy and historically accurate—with your Gen Zer, make sure that your child has all the necessary tools to see the truth for themselves. Strive to present the gospel without overly complicated reasoning or overly spiritual language. That's particularly important when making sure that the conversation is at an age-appropriate level. You don't want to talk over your child's head to the point that he or she can't understand what you're saying.

— — —

Though the incident took place several years ago, I can still remember the moment clearly. I was teaching a weekly apologetics class with the late Dr. Norman Geisler. After we wrapped up one of our sessions, a couple approached us. They were a bit withdrawn and looked as though they had just come from a battlefield.

Dr. Geisler cracked a joke to help break the ice. I can't remember the joke, but I recall that the couple chuckled.

"Are you two enjoying the class?" I asked.

"Oh, yes," said Terry, the wife. "We have thoroughly enjoyed the lectures. This is the first time we've ever learned about making a case for Christianity. It's been very eye-opening."

"But we do have a question," added Terry's husband, Ron. "How do we go home and teach what we're learning to our kids—especially to our oldest, who is in college and says that all religions are a bunch of nonsense?"

Dr. Geisler looked over as if he wanted me to give the parents some hope. I glanced down at the floor and asked God for the wisdom to encourage this defeated-sounding couple.

"The first thing I want to point out," I said, "is that you are both here learning about Christianity because you care about and love God's truth. Right?"

Ron and Terry nodded in agreement.

"But now is the true test: You need to take what you've learned in this class and find ways to share it with your children, especially your son in college."

Sadly, interactions like this one are increasingly common in the churches where I teach. Countless parents believe in God, trust Jesus Christ as Savior, and rely on the Bible as the Word of God, yet they lack the knowledge and skill to adequately articulate *why* they believe to their children.

That's why I'm going to present some ways to talk to your kids about God, Jesus, and the Bible—so that you can faithfully equip your children to believe in Christianity with confidence.

Talking to Your Gen Zer about God

Christian parents tend to assume that their children have a proper understanding of God, but that's not always the case. Many teens and college students have a distorted or negative view of God. Maybe they haven't received proper teaching about God, or perhaps they've picked up a few wrong opinions along the way. Others feel distant from God because they feel unworthy.

The first thing I want to say is that we should all try to be patient and avoid making assumptions about our kids.

Second, you don't need a theology degree to talk to your kids about God. If you do want to sharpen your knowledge, there are lots of resources available for parents, as well as plenty of passages in the Bible about the nature of God.

Third, a great way to start the conversation with your kids is by asking them some simple questions to get a feel for what they know (or don't know) about the topic:

- "Who do you think God is?"
- "What do you know about God?"
- "What does the Bible say about God?"
- "Why can't we see God?"
- "Are there ways we can know that God is with us?"

In a church survey I conducted, seventeen-year-old Caleb expressed his view of God in these terms: "God, to me, is like a mighty being who I feel is never pleased with how I live my life."

Jessica, an eighth grader, described God as a "distant and cold deity who cares nothing about us."

What might be a few good questions to ask a young person like Caleb or Jessica? Here are a few suggestions:

- "Caleb, why do you feel that God is disappointed with you? Has something happened to make you feel this way?"
- "Jessica, what do you mean when you refer to God as a 'cold deity'?"
- "Caleb, have you ever read through the Bible to learn what it teaches about God? Would you like to know what the Bible says about Him?"
- "Jessica, how and why did you develop the belief that God is distant?"

Most Christian children are taught that God is love (1 John 4:8). But God is also holy, righteous, and just (Psalm 22:3; Isaiah 5:16).

They need to know that God is both infinitely loving and unlimited in His goodness. He will never do something that goes against His nature. God cannot lie or do evil things.

Some Gen Zers Still Believe

"God is the creator of the universe who is the protector over us. He is my friend, my holy Father, and I can tell Him anything."

Breanna, 16

"Without God there is nothing. No life, no breath, no joy, no peace, no laughter, no beauty. Nothing. Without Him, we would be lost, sad, and broken all the time. Personally, I know exactly what that feels like, and it's a horrible place to be. So to me, God is beautiful. God is my everything."

Kaylee, 21

"Everything that I have and everything that I love is because of God. I am truly grateful and blessed that I know deep down that God loves me and my life belongs to Him. Jesus, who is God, is my Savior. He saved me from my sins and brought comfort, protection, security, love, and so much more to me."

Keziah, 15

"He is the one and only true God, who created the universe. God is the King of kings. He is omnipotent, omnipresent, and omniscient. Not only did He speak the world into existence, but He also formed man from the dust of the earth. When man strayed from perfect union with the Father, it separated us from Him. Because of His grace, God made a way to reconcile us to Himself through the sacrifice of His Son, Jesus, so that we can live in relationship with Him, both now and for eternity in Heaven."

Myah, 16

Fourth, look for regular opportunities to continue discussions about God. Go deeper with your older Gen Zers by examining proper theology about God. For example, bring up how the Bible teaches that God is one in nature (Deuteronomy 6:4; Isaiah 44:6-8; Galatians 3:20), yet He is also revealed in three distinctive (yet united) persons: Father, Son, and Holy Spirit. According to Hebrews 6:17-18, God is perfect and unchanging. That means God doesn't need to improve on who He is. He doesn't need to get better.

If your Gen Z children claim to be atheists, here are four proofs for them to consider about the existence of God. These are not exhaustive and are somewhat abbreviated for the sake of space. (Consider consulting some additional resources in the Notes at the end of this book.[12])

1. The first proof is *divine design*. Paul writes in Romans 1:20, "His invisible attributes, namely, his eternal power and divine nature, have been clearly perceived, ever since the creation of the world, in the things that have been made. So they are without excuse." Elsewhere, the Bible speaks to the universe's vast splendor and complexity, pointing to a magnificent Creator who made all things (Psalm 19:1-4).

2. The second proof is that *God has revealed Himself through human conscience*. God, who created the universe and placed the earth in orbit, also designed human beings to fulfill His purpose and gave us moral standards to live by. The Bible states that God's law is written on our hearts (Romans 2:14-15), which explains why we instinctively know right from wrong and have a moral obligation to do right.

3. The third proof for God's existence is *the person of Jesus Christ*. Jesus came into the world not only to reveal His love for humanity but to restore us to Himself by laying down

His life for our sins (1 Peter 3:18) and rising from the dead on the third day (Luke 24).

4. The fourth proof for God is found in *the Holy Scriptures.* Composed over a span of about sixteen hundred years, across three continents, and with forty different authors writing in three languages, the accuracy and coherence of the Bible are unmatched.

WHAT ABOUT EVIL?

Regarding the problem of evil, parents need to be able to give a reasonable and biblical defense. Here are three points you can use to make a case for the coexistence of God and evil.

1. Teach your kids that in the beginning, God created everything good. And because free will is a good thing, this means that mankind had the potential to choose wrong— to choose evil. It was Adam and Eve who freely chose to sin, resulting in evil entering the world. Therefore, God is not the author of evil. No, evil is the absence of good. Good and evil are like light and darkness. Darkness, simply put, is the absence of light.

2. Help them understand how inconsistent atheism is. For instance, what is an atheist's basis for morality? How can the atheist believe in objective right or wrong without some underlying standard of justice? If there is no God, then the atheist's beliefs about morality are subjective, not objective. By saying this, you are not putting down the atheist. You are merely revealing his or her inconsistent reasoning.

3. The final point is that God (despite what atheists believe) is *omnibenevolent*—possessing perfect or unlimited

goodness—not *malevolent*, and He will eradicate evil from the world one day. God knows the transience of sin and has His reasons for allowing it to run its course. For instance, as Joseph told his brothers in Genesis 50:20, "You meant evil against me, *but* God meant it for good" (emphasis added).

Thus, for an atheist to say that evil exists because God is malevolent is simply a false proposition—one that doesn't consider who God is or recognize that giving His children the freedom to choose their own actions essentially guarantees the existence of evil. At least the Bible explains exactly how sin entered the world and how God will remove it someday—something the atheist cannot do (see Acts 3:21; Romans 8:18-22).

Talking to Your Gen Zer about Jesus

Most kids love comic books and the movies based on them. Why is that? Because kids love superheroes. Guess who is the ultimate superhero? I'll give you a hint—it's not Captain America or Thor.

There is no other figure in history as remarkable, or as powerful, as Jesus Christ. He is not only central to faith and Christianity—Jesus is central to life! He wasn't just a wise man who did good deeds and said nice things. He came into the world as God in human form—the second person of the triune Godhead, the one who gave up His life to save the rest of us.

Check out these extraordinary facts to share with your kids:

- Jesus existed before the beginning of the world (John 1:1-3; 3:13; Hebrews 1:2).
- He was born in approximately 4 BC from a virgin mother (Isaiah 7:14; Daniel 9:24-26; Luke 1:26-56).
- He was born in Bethlehem (Micah 5:2; Matthew 2:1-11) and grew up in Nazareth in Galilee (Luke 2:39-40).

- He is both fully God and fully man (Matthew 16:16-17; John 8:56-59).
- He lived a sinless life (Matthew 27:4, 19, 23-24; Luke 23:13-15, 41; John 18:38).
- He performed many miracles (Matthew 9:18-30; 12:9-13).
- He fulfilled prophecy (Isaiah 9:6-7; 53:11; Daniel 9:25-26).
- He forgave people of their sins (Mark 2:1-12; Luke 5:17-26).
- He accepted worship from His followers (Matthew 8:2; 9:18; 14:33; 28:9, 17; John 9:38).
- He was betrayed, arrested, illegally tried, and crucified on a cross (Matthew 26–27; Mark 14–15; Luke 22–23; John 18–19).
- He was buried in a tomb for three days (Matthew 12:40; 28:1; 1 Corinthians 15:4).
- He physically rose from the dead (1 Corinthians 15:3-8) and appeared to His followers for forty days, teaching them about His Kingdom (Acts 1:3).
- He ascended *bodily* into heaven (Acts 1:9-11) and told His disciples that the Holy Spirit would empower them to spread His message to all nations (Matthew 28:18-20; Acts 1:8).
- He promised His followers that He would return one day (John 14:3).

Remind your kids that there is no one like Jesus. Take time to explore with them all Jesus' amazing stories, teachings, and miracles. If you're not sure where to begin, there are many free Bible reading plans you can do together as a family. It doesn't have to be a complicated plan; just make sure to discuss the readings with your kids regularly. (Daily is ideal.)

Another thing you can do to foster engaging family conversations about Jesus is to watch *The Chosen* series together.

Make time to explore the Gospels with your children and learn more about the life, death, and resurrection of Jesus Christ. The more your children learn about Jesus, the more their lives will change for the better.

Talking to Your Gen Zer about the Bible

One of the leading reasons why so many Gen Zers walk away from the Christian faith is that they don't believe the Bible is divine or true. Much of Gen Z believes that the Bible is an ancient book filled with errors, bigotry, and even lies. I've hung out with countless Gen Zers who say they never learned why the Bible can be trusted. Much of what kids and teens received in Sunday school or youth group was circular reasoning: "The Bible is true because it's the Bible." But that doesn't offer the evidence or the assurance that Gen Z needs.

Your Gen Z kids need to know *with certainty* that they can trust in and live according to the instructions found in the Bible. Here's an easy way to do just that by using the acronym *BIBLE*:[13]

1. *Brand:* There are all sorts of different brands, such as Honda automobiles, Apple iPhones, and Adidas shoes. The Bible has its own brand too, and it's a divine one. A remarkable feature of the Bible is the tremendous continuity between and within the biblical accounts of Creation, the Fall, mankind's redemption through Christ, and the final consummation of the new heaven and new earth. This high level of accuracy represented in sixty-six books written by forty different authors—whose occupations included peasant, prophet, fisherman, statesman, poet, plowman, doctor, and king—is simply extraordinary (2 Peter 1:20-21).

2. *Inspiration:* Christians believe the Bible is *divinely inspired,*

a term that comes from the Greek words *theos* ("God") and *pneustos* ("breathed"). When combined, the two words form *theopneustos*, which essentially means "God-breathed." This terminology is found in 2 Timothy 3:16: "All Scripture is *breathed out by God* and profitable for teaching, for reproof, for correction, and for training in righteousness" (emphasis added). Jesus said, "Every word . . . comes from the mouth of God" (Matthew 4:4) and "cannot be broken" (John 10:35). That's how innately powerful the Word of God is! When you read or hear teaching from the Bible, it's like experiencing the very breath of God.

3. *Background:* Early leaders of the Christian church used specific criteria to identify God's inspired books: (1) Was it written by a prophet (spokesperson) from God? (2) Was the author confirmed as a prophet of God, whether by miracles or other means? (3) Is it consistent with other revelations and truths contained in other inspired books? (4) Does it reveal the life-changing power of God? (5) Has the church always accepted and taught its truths? These questions acted as a guide to officially recognize (canonize) the books of the Bible and ensure that each one, from Genesis to Revelation, aligned doctrinally.

By the first century AD, Jewish leaders had accepted all the Old Testament books as parts of God's Word. By the end of the fourth century, early church leaders at the Synod of Hippo and the Council of Carthage decreed that the twenty-seven books of the New Testament were divine Scripture. (It wasn't the church leaders who made the New Testament books authoritative—they merely confirmed that these works were divinely inspired.)

4. *Literature:* The Bible has more early, abundant, and accurately copied manuscripts than any other text from the ancient world. There are more than eight thousand recorded manuscripts of the New Testament in the original Greek. These manuscripts are among the oldest surviving documents from the ancient world, and they are more than 99 percent accurate. In fact, 100 percent of all the primary teachings of the Bible are conveyed in these early copies.

5. *Errorless Teaching:* While there are some minor errors (mainly misspellings) in the early copies of the Bible, there are no errors in any significant teachings. Many of the Bible's writers were either eyewitnesses to the events or contemporaries of eyewitnesses (Luke 1:1-4; Hebrews 2:3-4), and many archaeological discoveries have since verified these historical accounts. Luke mentions dozens of details in the book of Acts alone that are supported by more modern discoveries.

So as you discuss the Christian faith with your children, try to get them thinking for themselves. Ask them some tough questions. Read materials that provide evidence for God's existence and talk about them together. Don't just assume what your kids know or believe. Avoid the "that's just your opinion" response by backing up your beliefs with evidence.

At the same time, you don't need an advanced theological degree to help teach your children. Just relax and ask God to help you. I know some parents who get so worked up over the mere thought of talking about faith and the Bible that they tend to avoid opportunities altogether. Trust me—the more you initiate these conversations, the more relaxed and routine they will become.

Parenting Practice

1. Be Aware of Spiritual Warfare

Spiritual warfare is real. Satan is a real, cunning foe who operates with great deception. He attacks the truths of God with lies, floods the mind with doubts, and tempts the heart to sin. The primary purpose of Satan's attacks is to undermine our relationship with God.

The apostle Paul warns Christians to "put on the whole armor of God, that you may be able to stand against the schemes of the devil. For we do not wrestle against flesh and blood, but against the rulers, against the authorities, against the cosmic powers over this present darkness, against the spiritual forces of evil in the heavenly places" (Ephesians 6:11-12).

At the heart of many secular beliefs and worldly behaviors prevalent among Gen Z is spiritual warfare. Satan is largely responsible for spreading false ideas, worldviews, and lifestyles that run contrary to the Christian faith, and he takes advantage of the human appetite for sin.

Therefore, you and your spouse (if you are married) need to be watchful for Satan's spiritual attacks against you and your family (1 Peter 5:8).

2. Address Your Kids' Doubts

Here are a few questions for you: What are some of the doubts that your child is facing right now? How often have they brought them up? What are you doing or what have you done to help them? Are you concerned about these doubts? Why or why not?

By the time a child reaches, say, ten years old, he or she

will have likely developed a few doubts about who they are and what they believe. Yet out of fear or confusion, your kids may not express those doubts openly. It's important to tell them that it's perfectly normal to struggle with doubt sometimes. What's not good is to ignore those thoughts and feelings. If your children brush aside or bury their doubts, those doubts will likely weaken their faith or even prompt them to abandon their beliefs altogether.

So take the time to introduce stories about people of faith who struggled with doubt. Let your child know about when Moses doubted God (Exodus 5:22-23) or when John the Baptist doubted Jesus (Luke 7:18-23). The point is to show young people that some of the greatest figures in Scripture struggled with doubt from time to time. Let your teens and tweens know that one of Satan's strategies is to target their doubts, attacking any certainty they have about God and replacing it with uncertainty. That's his goal, so make it your goal to help them understand that God is faithful and will never leave or forsake them. As Deuteronomy 32:4 says, "The Rock, his work is perfect, for all his ways are justice. A God of faithfulness and without iniquity, just and upright is he."

3. Teach Your Kids to Test What They Believe

What do you think is required before an experimental drug can be marketed to the public as an approved treatment for cancer? It typically takes years of rigorous testing to demonstrate that the treatment is both safe and effective.

Christianity is all about "testing" any and all teachings to determine what is right and good (1 Thessalonians 5:21). Likewise, for your Gen Zers to know what they believe is true, they should learn to test it for themselves.

Here are three fundamental questions that you and your child should ask:

- *Are there any contradictions in what we believe?* For a statement or belief system to be logically consistent, it must not contradict itself.
- *What evidence is there to support our claims or beliefs?* An intellectually honest pursuit of truth will reveal if your belief can withstand historical, philosophical, and rational inquiries. If what you believe is true, your claims will be backed up by evidence.
- *How does a particular belief line up with life itself?* Take driving directions, for example. It matters a great deal to have the right directions in order to reach your destination. If you input the wrong address, a GPS device will lead you to the wrong location. Similarly, your children need to make sure that their spiritual beliefs are taking them in the right direction in life.

6

CHALLENGING CONVERSATIONS TO HAVE WITH YOUR KIDS ABOUT SEX, GENDER IDENTITY, AND PORN

KIDS SAY THE DARNDEST THINGS, don't they? You never know what's going to come out of their mouths next.

When my daughter Amy was six or seven years old, she was sitting with her mother and me in church while the pastor taught about Solomon's life—including the many concubines he had as king. Later that day, as my wife prepared dinner, Amy looked up from her coloring book.

"Mommy?" she said.

"Yes, my dear?" Celia responded.

"Are you daddy's concubine?"

You should have seen the look on Celia's face. My first reaction was to bust out laughing, yet the thought of discussing a concubine's role with my little girl quickly turned my laughter into panic.

In hindsight, that discussion was a cakewalk compared with

the more serious and challenging conversations we face with our kids today.

A NECESSARY EVIL

When was the last time you had a difficult conversation about a tough topic with one of your kids? How did it go? Were you prepared? Did your answers help or hurt the situation?

As Gen Zers get older, they often develop views and adopt positions counter to what you've taught them to believe. It's not uncommon to hear about elementary-age kids disagreeing with their parents on matters of religion, or teens insisting that their current identity differs from their gender "assigned" at birth.

My friend Tony knows this all too well.

When his daughter was younger, Tony never made any effort toward—or saw the value in—talking to her about controversial issues. Over dinner not long ago, he told me that as his daughter matured, so did her views on evolution, sexuality, religion, and social justice issues. At one point during our conversation, Tony dropped his fork on his plate and gave out a big sigh.

"You know what's so sad, Jason?" he asked.

"What's that, Tony?"

"I don't even know how to talk with my daughter anymore," he said. "I've tried everything, but all she wants to do is argue with me and tell me I'm a religious fanatic and anti-gay. It's people like me who are ruining America with my intolerant views. She's so much like her mother—and that relationship, of course, didn't work out in the end."

After taking in everything Tony shared, I asked him one question: "Tony, do you think if you had invested more in your daughter when she was younger, things might be different between you two?"

I paused a few seconds to let that sink in. He eventually mustered enough of a reaction to concede my point.

"You need to humble yourself and learn to listen to your daughter," I continued. "You don't need to raise your voice every time she says something you disagree with. Focus more on relating to your daughter before jumping into a heated conversation that ends up with the two of you arguing."

Maybe you and your Gen Z child are at an impasse over some tough topics. Perhaps the two of you can't seem to accept each other's point of view. If so, you are not alone. Whatever the reason, Gen Z seems to have a hard time talking to their parents about controversial issues. They also have a hard time asking adults for help or seeking their advice. I have found three primary reasons why Gen Z avoids engaging their parents on various matters of opinion:

- They are intimidated by the subject matter or concerned that discussion might lead to disagreement.
- They lack faith or trust in the source (i.e., their parents) giving them the information.
- They are simply unwilling to listen to views that run contrary to their own.

Regardless of their reasons, your children *need* you to maintain communication with them. They need you to take the lead and initiate conversations. They will always have questions (don't we all?), and they will always need answers. They may not like some of your answers, but they will usually appreciate your sharing them. Too often parents miss the opportunity to dispel false information. It's not always about getting your kids to agree with you. It's more often about letting them discover what you stand for and why. Keep in mind that disagreeing with you doesn't mean they don't respect you.

Challenging conversations are a necessary evil. We may not relish them, but they are unavoidable at times. Don't look for an escape hatch to avoid talking to your kids about what's going on in their world. You will likely have a tough conversation if your child has been exposed to something inappropriate, offensive, or controversial. You're right to be concerned, but don't overreact. You can still take steps to help shield your child from harmful influences and counter those same influences using the Word of God.

Opening the doors of dialogue with your kids should help you understand how they perceive various topics and why, give you insight into their sensitivity regarding some issues, and provide you with a clearer perspective on how to move forward. Your kids need to feel safe when sharing their feelings and viewpoints. One of the quickest ways to shut down communication is to demonstrate that you are not a safe person, and nothing demonstrates that faster than making your child feel shame and judgment. Modern culture has already distorted God's truth about marriage, sex, and gender, so if you want to speak to those sensitive issues with your kids, then you need to be a safe haven and a trusted source.

For the record, you won't be able to effectively tackle tough topics through one-and-done conversations. More likely, you will need to have ongoing discussions with your kids as they get older.

THE CHALLENGING CONVERSATION ABOUT SEX

Talking to kids about human anatomy and explaining where babies come from isn't a discussion that most parents look forward to.

I'm reminded of a time when a young couple approached me after church. I'll never forget the expression on the man's face—by the looks of it, I figured they were having a marital dispute and needed some counsel. The wife gestured to her husband, who was struggling to find the right words.

"My wife wants me to have the 'sex talk' with our boys," he finally said, "but I don't know what to say. I was hoping you could help us."

Definitely not what I was expecting. But I'm going to let you in on a little secret: It's typical for parents to feel uneasy when it's time to have "the talk." Many parents feel how this father felt when it comes to discussing sex and sexuality with their kids.

The first thing I tell parents to do is relax. There's no need to panic. A big reason why we get so uncomfortable talking about sex and sexuality is the negative stigma associated with it. Too many people in the church would rather avoid the topic.

Why is that? After all, it's God who created us as sexual creatures. It's God who made sex a good thing, and it's God who designed it to be a shared pleasure between a husband and wife. We shouldn't lose sight of that truth. What we need are more parents willing to educate their children on the proper place of sex in marriage. If parents are too afraid to talk about sex with their kids, then who will teach them? Yeah, that's right. They will learn about it from a culture that ignores God and has twisted the meaning and purpose of sex.

Here are just three examples of how school systems today teach our kids about sex:

- Parents in Hudson, Ohio, discovered a textbook prompting high school students to "write a sex scene you wouldn't show your mom."[1]
- Two Texas middle-school libraries offered a young adult novel that describes anal sex.[2] The school board removed the book after parents complained, but who approved the book in the first place?

- In a prestigious New York private school, parents learned
  that their first graders were shown animated videos that
  talked about masturbation.[3]

I know these stories are troubling, and I wish I didn't have to mention them. But this is the reality of raising Gen Z. No matter where
Gen Z goes—or what they read, view, or click—the predominant
cultural message is that they are free to express their sexuality however they see fit.

— — —

When I first broached the subject with my third child, Jackson—
he was about seven years old at the time—I took him out for
burgers and milkshakes. (I particularly love a good mint chocolate
chip shake!) That's because I've learned that a fun meal with your
kid can help reduce awkwardness.

As Jackson and I chomped down on our burgers in the car, I
started in Genesis and described how God created the first couple:
Adam and Eve. From there, I asked my son about some of the
differences he noticed between his mom and me. I didn't want
to overwhelm him with too much (or too graphic) information.
So I gently eased him into learning about how sex organs differ
between boys and girls.

Feeling full (and a bit wired from the shake), we wrapped up
our first sex talk by discussing the special love that his mother and
I share as a married couple.

Not long after that first talk, Jackson and I picked up where we
left off with an age-appropriate lesson about how babies come into
the world. I shared with Jackson that God designed sex as a beautiful gift for married couples—a gift that involves both pleasure and
procreation. I told him that as he got older, his body would start

developing, and something inside him called *hormones* would play a big role in his physical, emotional, mental, and sexual maturity. I reassured him that all this was perfectly normal, that we all go through this process as we get older. But if he ever started to experience something weird or unfamiliar, then he should let me know. Finally, I told him that if we ever needed to make an appointment with his pediatrician to make him feel better about these changes, we would do that.

Notice how I introduced the topic of sex with my son and the way I went about it. I kept it on a level that made sense to him, and I did my best to make him feel safe.

--- --- ---

When it comes to having "the talk" with your kids, it's important to keep their age and stage of life in mind. We want to make sure those discussions are appropriate yet informative, respecting their curiosity about sexual desires and helping preserve their innocence along the way.

Another thing to keep in mind when talking about sex with your kids: It's almost never a good idea to tell your kids to *suppress* their sexual desires. Instead, help them better understand those desires and how to *control* them (see Galatians 5:17-25). They need to know that many influences in the culture will attempt to shape their sexuality in ways that don't align with God's design. And as you speak with your kids, always point them back to God—the ultimate standard of holiness.

Make sure your teens understand that God's restriction on sex outside marriage isn't to oppress them; rather, it's a mandate of protection. Pastor and blogger Tim Challies puts it this way: "Our sexuality is a gift given to us in trust. We are to steward it faithfully, to use it in the ways God commands and to refuse to use it in the ways he forbids."[4]

Yet many young people behave as if they are invincible. They've become convinced that what they do with their bodies during their teenage years will have few or no consequences for their adult years. That's why it's incumbent on you as parents to challenge the leading Gen Z perspective regarding sexual intercourse outside marriage. As more Gen Zers embrace moral relativism as a license to express their sexual freedom, more of their generation will become numb to the consequences of their actions.

Depending on the age of your children, don't shy away from discussing the consequences of sex outside marriage. Let them know about the potential for sexually transmitted infections (HIV, chlamydia, genital herpes, gonorrhea, syphilis, and others), the pain of breakups, the risk of unplanned pregnancy, and the truth about abortion.

Be sure, however, to explain that God's design for sex isn't just a list of *don'ts*. Teach your children about God's love and grace and how we are to use our bodies to glorify Him. All of us are made in God's image and likeness (Genesis 1:27) and have been endowed with spiritual, emotional, and intellectual abilities that reflect God in unique and special ways. Humans are God's most cherished creation in that we alone were created in His image.

We are raising our children in a time when their generation has accepted the idea that sexual orientation, even gender, is a fluid state that can change from day to day. Their generation has embraced the notion that sleeping with whomever they desire on Tinder is no big deal. That's why it's up to us, as parents, to work with our spouses (and yes, your ex if you're divorced) to model and teach our kids about modesty, chastity, and fidelity.

A good exercise to engage in before every tough talk with your kids is to reflect on the kinds of discussions you had with your parents. What were some of the talks you remember the most? What do you wish they had told you? Repeat what worked, and learn from what didn't. And whatever you do, do *something*. Remember, if you don't talk to your kids about sex, they will learn about it *somewhere*, and it's likely to be from someone who doesn't share your perspective.

THE CHALLENGING CONVERSATION ABOUT GENDER IDENTITY

Not long ago, a mother approached me after an event to share some frustrations she had with her daughter. The woman's name was Jenny, and she told me that her daughter was challenging her biblical views of marriage.

"What are some of her challenges?" I asked.

"Well," said Jenny as she mused aloud, "my daughter told me that Adam and Eve never existed and that Jesus never condemned same-sex marriage. She is always sending me YouTube videos that are pro-gay and attack the Bible. I've gotten to a point where I don't know how to answer her anymore."

What do you say to your kids when the conversation turns to same-sex attraction (SSA) or gender dysphoria/confusion? What about when your son or daughter tells you that they struggle with SSA or gender dysphoria? Where do you begin?

Let me first say that processing these sorts of issues with your child is never easy, but you and your child can get through this with God's help. And if you find out your child deals with SSA, don't automatically assume that he or she is gay or a lesbian. Most importantly, make sure your child knows that you love him or her and that you want to do whatever you can to help.

For your child's sake, maintain your composure and focus on listening as you discuss how long your son or daughter has been feeling this way. You might feel the urge to interrupt or challenge them as they share, but that will typically make matters worse. Your job is to listen and pray. You can't "fix" your children from the outside. Start by working to understand their feelings from the inside. This applies whether they are experiencing SSA or gender dysphoria.

In a nonconfrontational way, try asking your son or daughter a few questions:

- "How long have you felt this way?"
- "Is this the first time you've acknowledged your SSA or gender dysphoria?"
- "Have you talked to God about these feelings?"
- "What do you need from me?"
- "Are you looking for help in dealing with these feelings? If so, in what way?"

Remember to keep the discussion focused on the *person* (who your child is in Christ) and not on sexual *orientation* or gender *identity* (the desires or confusion he or she is feeling). Three primary areas you want to help strengthen in your child are (1) their emotional state, (2) their spiritual state, and (3) their social state. You want to invest in helping them shape their identity as a child of God; in turn, this will give them a proper framework for their sexuality and gender identity. But only Jesus can truly transform them and give them real peace and joy.

An important distinction here is the difference between *acceptance* and *approval*. As a Christian parent, you are called to *accept* your children no matter what. They are your flesh and blood. However, that doesn't mean you must *approve* of every choice regarding their sexual expression. But as mentioned earlier, try to avoid jumping to conclusions. Some young people experience SSA or gender confusion, but that doesn't mean they will immediately or permanently identify as gay, lesbian, or transgender. In many cases, kids who are initially confused about their gender or sexuality will later resolve that confusion.

Our society tells our children that they don't need to accept the gender or sex they were "assigned" at birth. For example, if you are a woman who wants to transition into a man, society tells you that you have the right to determine your identity. That is why Jonathan, a junior in high school, says his friend Tammy can determine her gender or sex. In fact, Jonathan was somewhat exasperated by his father's belief in gender binarism (that gender consists of just two forms—male and female).

"Dad, my friend Tammy, who self-identifies as a man, has every right to make that determination," Jonathan stated.

"I realize that you and I don't see eye-to-eye on LGBT matters," replied Jonathan's father, Jack. "But I do want you to know that doesn't mean I don't love people in the LGBT community."

"Yeah, sure, Dad. Whatever."

Jack pulled up a seat next to his son. "I just wanted to make that clear," he said, "because if I happen to present an argument against transgenderism, that doesn't mean I'm narrow-minded or transphobic."

Here are a few responses that parents (like Jack) might use with their pro-LGBT kids:

- "You say that sexuality defines a person's identity. What evidence do you have to back up your claim?"

- "How do our desires or attractions define who we are? Being attracted to someone simply describes a sexual desire or a level of emotional engagement. There is much more to males and females than just their sexuality."

- "I'm having trouble understanding how the LGBT community defines identity. According to those who identify as lesbian, gay, or bisexual, they are defined by their attraction or sexual desires. But most trans-identifying people say their identity is *not* based on attraction or even gender. They say it's based on how they *feel* about themselves. How can both be true?"

- "Gender neutrality and transgenderism run contrary to God's design. From the beginning, God created humans with two biological sexes, male and female, complementing one another. That is, a man and a woman are suitable for each other (Genesis 2:18, 20-23). To say that a person is merely 'assigned' a sex at birth contradicts biology. At the moment of conception, a person doesn't *achieve* a sex but *receives* a fixed set of chromosomes (either XY or XX). No matter how much a male feels like a female (or vice versa), he will always be genetically male. That's not bigotry; that's just the science of biology."

No matter how your conversations go, always try to keep the lines of communication open. And if necessary, seek out a biblical counselor who specializes in gender and sexual confusion. I also recommend looking into the stories of faithful men and women of God who once lived a gay or lesbian lifestyle or who experience SSA: Christopher Yuan, Sam Allberry, Rosaria Butterfield, and Becket Cook, to name a few.

THE CHALLENGING CONVERSATION ABOUT PORN

The grip that pornography has on this generation is unlike anything I have ever seen. It seems like almost every teen or college student I've ever spoken with has seen pornographic images, and many can't seem to break their Internet porn addiction.

In my book *Challenging Conversations*, I lay out several reasons why pornography is a hidden danger that few people want to discuss—a killer that destroys untold numbers of lives:

- It is accessible and private.
- It destroys the mind.
- It silences conversations because many people are embarrassed to talk about it.
- It has a stigma because many people feel guilty about viewing it.
- It masks stress and failure because many who consume porn do so to experience a sense of relief or escape.[5]

I shared with you earlier that the average age of exposure to Internet porn is thirteen, with some children exposed as early as five years old. The point is, Gen Z has easy access to porn, and the results aren't good. I have counseled many Gen Zers who are infatuated with hardcore porn and have a warped view of sex altogether.

Avoid beginning the conversation with your child by jumping immediately into the graphic nature of porn and why it's so bad. Instead, pray with your child first. Then take him or her back to the Garden of Eden in Genesis. Make sure your kids know that God created sex as a beautiful gift between a husband and a wife, but also help them understand that sex can be taken out of its proper context and abused. This might lead you to ask your kids what they know about porn.

Please pay close attention to the answer. Many times, your son or daughter will say that porn is wrong or inappropriate and that it doesn't honor God. You can certainly affirm that answer, but don't stop there.

Don't be afraid to ask your son or daughter if they have ever viewed porn. If you learn that your children have been exposed—and the research suggests that they probably have—then you can certainly ask how it happened. Maybe a friend showed them a nude picture on their phone, or maybe they received a message on social media that led them to a porn site. Or perhaps it was out of curiosity. Most kids know how to use the private web browser mode known as Incognito, which many people use to search for naked images or even sex videos. Once again, instead of launching into a lecture, the best thing for you to do is listen and let your child talk.

As you can imagine, there is a great deal of shame and embarrassment that comes with viewing porn. So go easy on your son or daughter. A great way to defuse their guilt is to remind your children that God's love is far greater than their sin (1 John 3:20). As you talk about God's grace and forgiveness, acknowledge that lots of people (maybe including you) experience sexual struggles. Talk about how others have found freedom from those struggles through the power of Christ.

Understanding the extent of your kids' porn exposure isn't so you can embarrass them. Sure, these might feel like hard questions, but their answers will help you know how to love and protect them. Yes, it's natural for your children to feel bad about their sin. Still, the goal is to help them seek the forgiveness of Jesus and to provide them with safeguards and accountability that will put them on the track to freedom.[6]

Let me just say that it likely won't happen overnight. It can sometimes take years to fully experience freedom from the addictive effects of porn. It often depends on the degree of porn consumption and the maturity of the individual, both spiritually and mentally. (Also consider seeking the services of a trained Christian counselor who has experience working with kids and teens in this area.)

But here's the good news: The more you model grace to your kids, the more willing they will be to come to you for advice and spiritual accountability.

Finally, let me repeat that these challenging interactions about sex, gender identity, and porn are not meant to be one-and-done conversations. It's up to you to keep the discussions going. Trust the Lord that He will use you to speak truth and life into your family as you encourage them to remain set apart for God's good purposes.

Parenting Practice

1. In this chapter, I listed three reasons why Gen Zers avoid engaging with their parents on controversial topics. Place each of your children's names in one of the three boxes that best explains why they might not want to open up to you.

INTIMIDATED OR SHY	LACKING TRUST	PRIDEFUL

2. Create three columns on a piece of paper. In the first column, list your children and their ages. In the next column, list the top five agreements you share with each child. Then, in the third column, list the top three disagreements you have with each child. Consider the reasons behind these agreements and disagreements.

3. What is one thing you can do to improve the way you talk to your kids about sensitive issues?

4. Discuss with your spouse or other parents what safeguards you've put in place to protect your kids from accessing pornography on the Internet. What can you do to improve those safeguards?

5. If you haven't yet spoken to your child about sex (and you know it's time), don't delay any longer. Share with him or her about the beauty of God's design for a husband and wife and the special gift of sex within the confines of marriage.

6. Plan a fun day trip or weekend getaway with each child (fathers with sons and mothers with daughters, if possible) that will be a special time for just the two of you to discuss the topic of sexual purity. Visit FocusOnTheFamily.com /wp-content/uploads/2019/08/The-Talk.pdf for some additional tips and resources.

CHALLENGING CONVERSATIONS TO HAVE WITH YOUR KIDS ABOUT DEPRESSION, SUICIDE, ABORTION, AND RACISM

"I DON'T KNOW HOW IT HAPPENED," said a friend. "But I've gotten hooked on watching a show called *Gold Rush* on Discovery+."

"Oh yeah?" I responded. "What's the show about?"

My friend described the great lengths that the gold miners on the TV show go to in search of the precious ore. I checked out a few episodes for myself, but I didn't get hooked.

One thing I could appreciate, however, was the painstaking work of these miners. And let me tell you, it is an arduous process. Mining requires an excavator to dig deep into the earth's surface to reach *pay dirt*—a mining term for earth that has ore in it and might contain gold—or even hit a lode of gold-bearing rock.

The show got me thinking. Much like digging deep in search of gold, parents need to dig deep when mining the depths of our kids' hearts. It's not always easy, and the process requires time and effort. Sometimes you'll reveal new areas of your child's heart. Other times you'll hit solid rock. Yes, your children might not open up at first, making it hard to uncover much of anything—but you keep on digging until you strike pay dirt!

We don't get there by nagging or pestering. We reach our children's hearts (the gold) by engaging them in ways that make them comfortable conversing openly with us.

As we discussed in the previous chapter, having challenging conversations with our kids is both healthy and necessary. That's why I added a second chapter dealing with additional difficult conversations on tough topics. In this chapter, I'll help equip you to properly and biblically manage talking with your kids about depression, suicide, abortion, and racism.

THE CHALLENGING CONVERSATION ABOUT DEPRESSION AND SUICIDE

There was a time when a child's mood swings were chalked up as nothing more than a phase—something that the child would soon grow out of. Today, however, significant mood swings can signal something far more precarious. They can indicate that your son or daughter suffers from depression or some other mental disorder.

That might sound surprising, but it's true. I know many Christians who battle depression but are too ashamed to share their struggles out of fear of being judged. Yet the issue isn't going away anytime soon: Gen Z is growing up in a time when one out of every four people suffers from some form of mental illness.[1]

I am reminded of a troubling conversation I had with a high school student after delivering a message on depression. There was no small talk with this young lady—she came right out and told me that she had attempted suicide a few months prior. (Thankfully, a school administrator who had been working with this child and her family was standing right next to me.) I was so impressed by the optimism and confidence this high schooler had in Christ. She explained that she knew God had saved her from dying because He loved her and had a special calling for her. That was awesome to hear. What wasn't so awesome to hear was that the student's mother doubted the sincerity of her daughter's Christian faith after her attempted suicide.

This wasn't the first time I'd heard about parents responding this way to their depressed child. And I must tell you, it is absolutely the wrong thing to say—especially if your child is trying desperately to hold on to their faith. Just because someone suffers from depression or has a mental illness—or has even attempted suicide—this doesn't mean he or she isn't a Christian. As a matter of fact, the prophet Elijah went so far as to beg God to take his life (1 Kings 19:4).

As discussed in chapter 4, young people often feel overwhelmed by the pressures of life. They feel the need to fit in, to make friends, to get good grades, and to succeed in sports or music or any number of activities. Add in the emotions associated with teenage relationships, and it's not hard to understand why so many kids struggle!

Another source of anxiety among Gen Z is how much control their parents have over their lives. Those Gen Zers who crave space and margin in their lives often experience ongoing conflict with parents who insist on too much oversight, authoritarianism, or just plain meddling in their personal lives. Keep this in mind if there is ongoing conflict with your child about spending too much time alone. Don't automatically assume that isolation is a sign of depression, but it might be. If the conflict or anxiety continues to get worse, or if you're concerned that your child might be depressed, it's always better to consult a trained counselor.

My wife and I attended the funeral of a man in his twenties who had taken his own life. The young man's mother shared how her son always felt the pressure to do things just right. It didn't matter how well he performed or the amount of praise he received; in his mind, he was never good enough. That desire for perfection ate away at her son over the years. I can't say for sure that the pressure he felt caused him to take his life, but I can't imagine that it didn't affect his decision.

I know this can be overwhelming for parents, too, so let's discuss how to recognize and respond to a child suffering from depression. Here are some steps you can take:

1. *Pray.* Psalm 34:17-18 tells us, "When the righteous cry for help, the Lord hears and delivers them out of all their troubles. The Lord is near to the brokenhearted and saves the crushed in spirit."

2. *Try to avoid technical terms.* Don't overload your child with too much scientific and medical information about depression. You can simply say that depression is like a sickness in the brain that makes a person feel really sad. Depressed people can feel exhausted, unmotivated, or even scared to do things or be around people. What you want your child to understand is that depression is more than just feeling bummed about something. Depression affects your physical and mental well-being. Some people describe it as living in a black hole.

3. *Explain what causes depression.* Let your child know that mental health problems can be brought on by many different reasons, and those reasons vary from person to person. But mental health problems are almost never the result of just one thing. Depression isn't *only* a spiritual, or psychological, or physical, or relational problem. It's often all the above. Avoid making it sound as if depression is one-dimensional.

Many depressed people need therapy with a professional counselor, as well as medication, to properly function in life. That's not to say they don't love God enough or don't have enough faith. Receiving treatment for depression is much like a person with diabetes taking insulin or a person with asthma using an inhaler.

Here are some questions to help guide your conversation:

- "How long have you been feeling this way?"
- "Is there anything specific that might have caused you to feel depressed?"
- "What kinds of thoughts have you been experiencing?"
- "How is your relationship with God?"
- "Does anything seem to ease your depression?"
- "What can I do to help you with your depression?"
- "Have you experienced any suicidal thoughts?"
- "Are you willing to get professional help if necessary?"

Remind your son or daughter that even though there are times when they feel down and lonely, God will not abandon them to their misery and discomfort. He is always there for us and will give us what we need to make it through each day. If the situation with your child is serious or even moving in that direction, do not hesitate to seek professional help right away!

THE CHALLENGING CONVERSATION ABOUT ABORTION

I remember the first time my wife took our children to an abortion clinic. (Yes, you read that correctly.) You might think we are crazy parents, but it was a powerful way to educate our kids about one of the greatest evils known to mankind—abortion.

That night after dinner, my kids shared what they had learned by watching their mom stand on the sidewalk outside an abortion clinic, offering to take the women who arrived to get a free ultrasound exam before proceeding with an abortion.

I believe that we have done our children a disservice by not proactively addressing the issue of abortion with younger generations. Early on, my wife and I decided not to shelter our children, but instead to disciple and encourage them to engage the world—even if this meant exposing them to places where an expectant mother goes to abort her unborn child.

The bad news is that only about 30 percent of Gen Z say abortion is morally wrong. This is an even lower percentage than millennials, who come in at about 58 percent. That is a significant drop in just one generation.[2]

Despite the declining percentage of pro-lifers among the young, here's the good news: Young people are overwhelmingly convinced that abortion is morally wrong *after* hearing a strong case for life.[3]

With that in mind, I'd like to present two different cases for life. The first case is crafted for younger kids, while the second case is a bit more advanced for the older ones. I am not writing this as a refutation of anyone's position, but as more of an explanation. Both cases are ways to help your children understand that being pro-life aligns with a biblical worldview.

The Case for Life for Younger Gen Zers

The Bible makes it clear that every human being is made in the image of God. Genesis 1:27 says, "God created man in his own image, in the image of God he created him; male and female he created them."

We also know, from science and medicine, that a mother is carrying a human life from the moment of conception. In other words, the fetus doesn't have to get older to *become* a human being—that's because, right from the start, it *is* a human being. As a fetus grows bigger and more developed, it never stops or starts being a baby—a *baby human* who can move and feel. In fact, Luke 1:44 reads, "The baby in my womb leaped for joy." Right there we are told that preborn babies are alive and can feel certain things.

Once you've shared that point with your child, ask your son or daughter if it's right to kill an innocent human being. They will almost certainly say no. It is morally wrong to take an innocent life. Then ask them whether the preborn baby in its mother's womb is an innocent human being. If they understood the information you presented, they should affirm that it is. Your final question is, "What does abortion do to that innocent baby's life?"

Please be sure to tread lightly when discussing the specifics about abortion. The notion of a mother aborting her preborn child can be confusing and disturbing for a young child to grasp. The goal is to educate your child in an age-appropriate way that every preborn baby is an innocent human being made in the image of God. Moreover, it is God who gives life value; thus every baby has a right to be born, not aborted.

The Case for Life for Older Gen Zers

Here is the pro-life reasoning I typically use when talking about abortion. This reasoning consists of two points and a conclusion:

Point #1: All human beings have intrinsic value.
Point #2: The preborn are human beings.
Conclusion: Therefore, the preborn have intrinsic value.

The first point, that *all human beings have intrinsic value*, simply states the widely held belief that every person has value, worth, and dignity. Sure, a few radical thinkers might challenge this statement, but most will agree that all human beings deserve an equal right to life.

That's because a person's intrinsic value isn't based on what he or she can do or perform, but rather on who they *are*—their personhood. That is to say, something has intrinsic value when it is valuable for what it *is* rather than what it *does*. For example, your child has value not because she is smart or has a lot of money. She has value because she is a human being. Her value isn't tied to some function she performs or characteristic she has. Nor does her value increase as she gets older. Your daughter's value is grounded in her humanity, right from the start.

The second point, that *the preborn are human beings*, is based on the scientific evidence that life begins at conception. According to the science of embryology, the human embryo—from its earliest moments—is a genetically distinct, living human being. When an ovum from a human female unites in conception with a sperm cell from a human male, the result is a human life. This zygote, or fertilized ovum, is not a horse or a chicken; it is distinctively human. It has all the necessary genetic material right from the start. As philosopher and author Francis Beckwith describes it, "The unborn are not potential persons but persons with great potential."[4]

When you consider and acknowledge these two points, it logically follows that *the preborn have intrinsic value*. If preborn babies are humans with intrinsic value, what does that say about abortion? It means abortion deliberately takes the life of an innocent human being. And since we've already acknowledged that killing innocent humans is morally wrong, there's no denying that abortion is morally wrong.

After making the case for life with your children, throw out some questions to see how they respond:

- If science indeed demonstrates that preborn babies are human, then which is more important—a baby's right to life or a woman's right to choose an abortion?

- Do you believe that your mother would have been morally justified if she chose to abort you during any stage of her pregnancy?

- Do you think it is a Christian's moral duty to stand up for the preborn?

Keep up the dialogue with your Gen Zers as they get older, and look for ways that your entire family can get involved in pro-life causes.

THE CHALLENGING CONVERSATION ABOUT RACISM

Let's face it: Racism is real and one of the main hot-button issues of our day. Considering all the tension surrounding the topic—including the rise of public demonstrations, concern about microaggressions, and public shaming of dissenting opinions—it's not surprising that some parents would rather avoid discussing racism with their kids.

Author and professor Andrew T. Walker expresses the discomfort quite pointedly: "Racial reconciliation is a sensitive subject with which well-meaning people feel intimidated to engage. It seems, at times, there are too many landmines and too many unforgivable sins in the discourse. But in order for us to grow together, we must not let the headwinds of complexity discourage a steady course toward reconciliation."[5]

Before delving deeper into the topic, let me acknowledge that there are many angles and approaches to talking about racism in our culture. For this book, I'll offer the following five points to help you guide the conversation and teach your kids how to both respect and honor others. Feel free to adapt the material to fit the uniqueness of your family. For those parents who've been marginalized, targeted by racial slurs, or made to feel inferior, your perspective will be far more personal than for those who have never experienced racism directly. Yet no matter our experiences, our responsibility as parents is to teach our children that racism is morally wrong and to stand up against racism through the power of forgiveness that comes only through Jesus Christ.

1. *God created* one *human race.* According to Genesis 1:27, "God created man in his own image, in the image of God he created him; male and female he created them." The apostle Paul declared, "And he [God] made from *one man every nation of mankind* to live on all the face of the earth, having determined allotted periods and the boundaries of their dwelling place" (Acts 17:26, emphasis added). God made one human race to populate the world, though that single race clearly manifests in different nationalities, languages, customs, and colors. The facts about a single race are also backed up scientifically. Modern science confirms that no matter their color or ethnicity, every single human being's DNA is 99.9 percent the same.[6] What does that mean? It means that although the world (and maybe even your family) is filled with different ethnic groups, we all still have the same basic genetic makeup as everyone else. We are all representatives of the one human race.

2. *Racism is morally wrong.* There are several reasons for this: (1) Racism rejects the universal, biblical truth that all humans are made in God's image and are therefore created

equal. (2) Racism promotes the misguided notion that some people groups are superior and thus have a right to oppress those people groups deemed inferior to them. (3) Racism is fueled by fear or hatred of others, and therefore it violates the dignity and intrinsic value that we all possess as God's most precious creation. (4) Racism is oppressive and disrupts the desired harmony among different nationalities and ethnic groups. (5) Racism directly violates Jesus' command to love everyone—from your neighbors to your enemies (see Mark 12:31; Luke 6:27-36).

3. *No children—or adults—should ever apologize for the color of their skin, their ethnicity, or even where they were born.* Whether your kids are brown, black, white, or anything else, they should never feel bad about their biological makeup or cultural background. They are who they are because God made them that way. No one should ever apologize for being born a different race, nationality, color, or gender.

4. *Every person deserves to be treated with dignity and respect.* It's essentially the Golden Rule: Treat others the same way that you wish to be treated (see Matthew 7:12). Everyone deserves to be treated with honor, if for no other reason than they bear the image of God. And while this certainly sounds right and good, the truth is that it doesn't always play out that way. The effects of racial bias are unavoidable. Talk openly with your children about people groups who have been oppressed.

A great example of someone to discuss with your Gen Zer is South Africa's first black head of state, Nelson Mandela. Mandela didn't end the country's system of apartheid and white rule through hatred, violence, and looting.

Instead, Mandela upheld justice and peace for South Africans by working with the very people who previously devalued him as a human being. Mandela knew that for his country to experience peace, he must rely on justice to prevail. So Mandela led the way in promoting solidarity. As James 3:18 tells us, "The fruit of righteousness is sown in peace by those who cultivate peace" (HCSB).

5. *It was God who created diversity among humanity.* God's image-bearers exhibit a wide variety of different skin colors and physical features. Instead of ignoring these distinctions or teaching our children to be "colorblind," the better course is to recognize and celebrate these differences among all people groups and to embrace God's beauty as represented across humanity. So encourage your children to befriend *all* people—including those who look or act different from them. And last but not least, discuss with your Gen Zers how they might engage the topic of racism on social media, as well as what forms of activism they support and why. Help them see which movements do the best job in campaigning for racial unity and reconciliation. Lots of groups advocate for equality, but if their methods include destruction and violence, then it's best to consider alternatives. Hatred and violent protests are not the best ways to bring about justice and unity.

Parenting Practice

1. If you have kids who are in eighth grade and up, I recommend reading my book *Challenging Conversations: A Practical Guide to Discuss Controversial Topics in the Church* with your kids. You can watch the corresponding video clips at ChallengingConversations.org/resources.

2. Familiarize yourself with the various worldviews your children encounter at school, online, and within their spheres of influence. Discuss with your spouse a plan for engaging in challenging conversations with your kids, and then put your plan into action!

3. Teach—and model—for your kids the practice of listening to other people's points of view. A helpful exercise is to have your kids come up with a list of people they disagree with and why. See if they can make a case for what they believe, and then help them fine-tune their reasoning.

4. Host a gathering of young people at your home to discuss some pressing topics: abortion, gender identity, porn, premarital sex, racism, and depression. Demonstrate that you are willing to listen, not just disagree.

5. If you have children sixteen years old and up, consider enrolling them in a summer session at Summit Ministries. (Check out summit.org.)

PART THREE

HOW TO "KEEP IT 100" WHILE RAISING

GEN Z

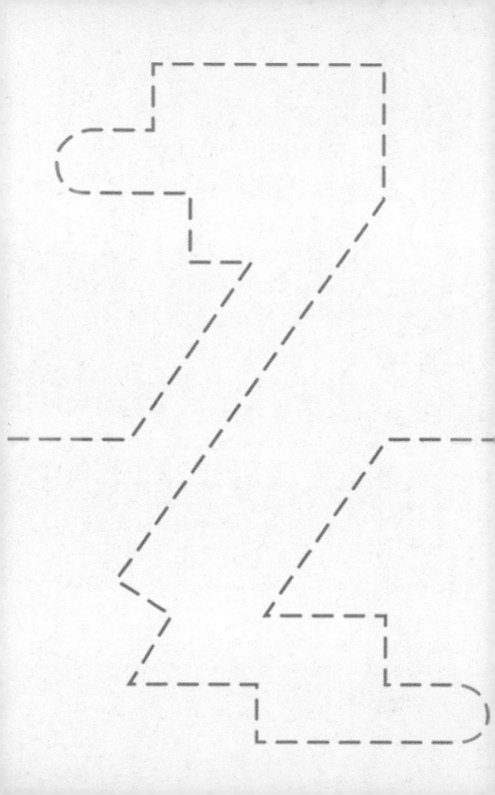

8

BUILD YOUR HOUSE ON *LOVE*

YEARS AGO, MY WIFE AND I BOUGHT a piece of land on which to build a bigger home as our family grew. This was our first new home build, so—needless to say—we were excited and nervous at the same time. Thankfully, the company we went with made the process of designing and building our new home a piece of cake. (If the blueprints and construction had been left up to me, our house might never have been completed!)

Just as my wife and I relied on experts to draw up the plans for our house, we need to rely on God's blueprints for the family. More often than not, parents raising Gen Z overlook their need for God's help and build their family the way *they* think it should be done. Before they know it, the family foundations are unstable, unbalanced, and falling apart. It's in these moments we are reminded that God is the optimal architect, not us.

For some of you, laying the appropriate groundwork for your

family might be something you did early on. Good for you! In that case, think of this section as a review. For others, this information is brand new. In either case, whether we're rookies or veterans, we all need reminders of God's divine design for the family and the special role He has given to parents. The biblical perspective on the family established in this chapter will be foundational as we move through the rest of part 3, addressing parental authority and making the adjustments necessary to spend more time with your family.

GOD'S BLUEPRINT FOR THE FAMILY

In the beginning, God formed man and woman and created for them the sacred and lifelong bond of marriage. The graphic below illustrates the family model established by God. Everything about the family, from the concept of love and the sacred bond of marriage to the joy of raising children—all of it, from start to finish—is God's divine design.

The sense of oneness found in marriage is a special relationship that beautifully expresses the unity shared among God the Father, God the Son, and God the Holy Spirit. That holy relationship is the model for our earthly marriages.

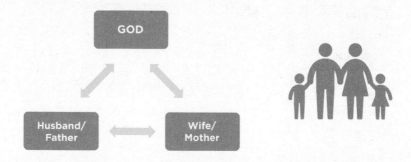

From the very beginning, parents have played a vital role in implementing God's standards and fulfilling His plans for families.

Parents don't always get it right, but as we confess our need for forgiveness, for guidance, and for the strength to persevere, our infinitely gracious God supplies us with exactly what we need.

In Ephesians 5:1-20, the apostle Paul clarifies how a Christian ought to live in the world. In Ephesians 5:21–6:4, he details what a Christian marriage and family ought to look like. You can see the progression in the chart below. Consider it another aspect of God's blueprint.

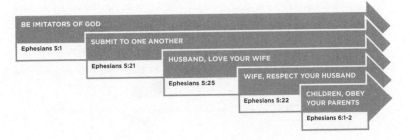

BE IMITATORS OF GOD
Ephesians 5:1

SUBMIT TO ONE ANOTHER
Ephesians 5:21

HUSBAND, LOVE YOUR WIFE
Ephesians 5:25

WIFE, RESPECT YOUR HUSBAND
Ephesians 5:22

CHILDREN, OBEY YOUR PARENTS
Ephesians 6:1-2

If you're a single parent, the challenges you face (as you are well aware) are often harder because you're on your own. It wasn't easy for my father to raise us four boys after my mother died. Yet God was there to give him the strength he needed to lead his family after our devastating loss. The same goes for other single parents. Ask God for a double portion of wisdom and strength so you can raise your children according to His Word and His blueprint.

If you are part of a blended family, then that, too, comes with its own set of challenges. Author and family therapist Ron Deal reminds stepparents of a powerful truth in Scripture. In an article for *Focus on the Family* magazine, Deal offers this insight: "Think about it: Jesus was raised by a stepdad. Certainly the circumstances surrounding His birth were—well—extraordinary. Being conceived by the Holy Spirit and born of a virgin certainly places His 'stepfamily' situation in a category of its own. Yet, when you stop to think about it, the God of the universe allowed His one and only Son to be raised by someone who wasn't His 'biological' father. My point: You are not alone."[1]

It doesn't matter if you and your spouse are raising your own biological kids, if you're a single parent, if you're remarried with stepchildren, or if you're an adoptive parent—the truth is that the best way to build a strong family is with God's help. King Solomon, a sage ruler, wrote in Psalm 127:1, "Unless the LORD builds the house, those who build it labor in vain."

Raising Gen Zers requires more than just googling some emergency parenting advice. With any family, you will experience challenges, arguments, mood swings, and hardships. But when your family's foundation is established on God (who is your Rock), no amount of rough weather can destroy it.

So how strong is your family's foundation?

BUILD YOUR FAMILY ON *LOVE*

As you can probably imagine, with six people in the Jimenez household, the family dynamics can get crazy at times. Yet despite all the hiccups, mix-ups, and messes that transpire in my home, I wouldn't want it any other way. Still, there eventually came a time when my wife and I were wondering if we (as parents) were doing all we could to have the most impact on our children's lives. The question boiled down to this: How could we be more intentional about ensuring that our family's foundation was based on God's Word?

That's how the *LOVE* acronym came about. It's my family's way to help remind all of us to (1) laugh together, (2) open up and share, (3) value one other, and (4) encourage each other every day.

Think of *LOVE* as a mission statement of sorts. Most successful companies have one, so why can't a family?

A mission statement is designed to reflect a particular set of values or principles, as well as the group's or organization's purpose. So when you choose to implement God's principles for your family, what's the best way to communicate those principles to the kids?

You can involve the entire family in developing a mission statement. When parents and children work together to establish clear and concise directives for the whole family to follow, things will be far less complicated and problematic. Of course, you as the parents have the final authority on your family's mission statement, but Gen Z kids are almost always more inclined to go along with things that make sense to them, too.

The *LOVE* concept made sense to our kids, and I hope it will to you and your family. Think of *LOVE* as both a motto and a mission statement offering you and your family practical ways to help you grow together. My wife and I can assure you that the *LOVE* concept has helped us raise our four Gen Z kids. I frequently run through the list to see if I've laughed with my kids, been open with them and them with me, shown them how much I value them, and encouraged them in some way recently.

I realize that your family is different from mine. Families come in all shapes and sizes. Whether we're married couples raising kids together, single parents, or blended families, we are all trying to do our best.

Whatever the makeup of your family, let's figure out how you can bring a little more *LOVE* into your home, based on God's divine design.

Laugh: Be Funny!

Fred Rogers, the iconic host of public television's *Mister Rogers' Neighborhood*, offered this simple reminder to pediatricians who wanted to communicate more effectively with their young patients: "You were a child once, too."[2] Mr. Rogers's advice applies to parents as well as pediatricians. I often encourage parents to lighten up and have more fun with their kids.

So let me ask you, Mom and Dad—do your kids think you're fun to be around?

A great way to have fun with your kids is to be a kid yourself. I'm not endorsing immature parenting; I'm encouraging parents to tap into Gen Z's imaginative personalities and learn what makes them laugh. I'll admit that I get a bit crazy with my kids sometimes, and that's when my wife feels like she's raising five children instead of four. But the point is that we have fun together.

Think back to when you were a child. What did you do for fun? Did you search for lost treasure in the backyard? Did you ride around the neighborhood on your bike, pretending to fight crime? Were you an imaginary pilot or a doctor or a princess or an athlete? Perhaps you were a world-class baker creating the tastiest cupcakes of all time out of Play-Doh.

Who were the people who made you laugh growing up? What activities were your favorites? The more you remember what it was like to laugh as a child, the more you'll look for fun and silly ways to engage with your kids, and the result will be more memorable times together.

In the Jimenez house, my kids love my dad jokes. (They really do!) I mean, come on, who doesn't enjoy a classic dad joke? And mine are the best in the world! Here's one for you: How did Darth Vader know what Luke got him for Christmas?

He felt his presence!

I'll wait until you're done laughing to continue.

The point is, you don't have to be a professional comedian to laugh together. And you don't need to spend a lot of money to have fun with your kids. I know I'm not a stand-up comic, but I can still tell my kids amusing stories about my childhood. I can play with them and make up silly characters. I can tell stories based on nothing but my imagination. If I'm not in a goofy mood myself, I can look up funny YouTube videos and we'll watch them together. And yes, I am that dad who rewatches the really funny parts—like five or six times. It drives my wife crazy!

What I'm trying to say is that the best time to start having fun with your kids is now!

Here are a few ideas to bring more laughter into your home:

- Play games as a family. There are countless games on the market, but you can always start with something simple (and cheap) like charades.
- Try impersonating famous people and evaluating who does the best impressions.
- Tell your kids about real-life characters from your childhood who made you laugh.
- Engage in some mild practical joking with your family members. (Be nice, dads!)
- Find some clean jokes online or in books that your family can read together around the dinner table.
- Send funny YouTube videos to the family via a group text.
- Find some good classic comedy movies that you can all watch as a family.
- Take turns each week coming up with a new fun activity.

Before you make excuses about being too tired or about your kids not wanting to do things together, remember that making excuses or not trying at all will only lead to your family drifting further apart. Don't let that happen. Don't miss out on having fun with your family.

I don't know who originally said it, but I feel like it's a good reminder for all of us: "Always find a reason to laugh. It may not add years to your life, but it surely will add life to your years."

Open: Be Vulnerable!

It's not uncommon for parents to hide their feelings and downplay what's going on in their hearts. This is especially true for dads. Many parents worry that opening up to others about a problem or expressing fear or regret can make them seem weak or unstable.

But you need to keep in mind that your kids—Gen Zers— aren't fooled. They know when something is wrong or when you're not telling them the whole truth. They may not know exactly what's going on, but they know when there's a problem.

There's actually great value in opening your heart to your kids—in letting them know they don't always have to have it all together:

- They feel closer to you on an emotional level.
- They are more likely to open up to you in return.
- They are less inclined to lie.[3]

Letting your kids know that you're having a bad day or sharing a mistake you made is a golden opportunity to speak openly to your children. Here are some examples:

- "I just want you to know that I am not feeling good right now and would appreciate your prayers."
- "I know I haven't been myself lately, and I'd like to tell you why."
- "You know, when I was about your age, I, too, was faced with a really tough decision . . ."
- "I've also been hurt by a friend. It wasn't easy, but it did teach me about trust. I tell you this because . . ."
- "Sweetie, I'm sorry for not being around much lately. Work is crazy busy right now. I'm not making excuses, but I love you and just want you to know that I miss spending time

with you. Maybe this weekend we can go do something just you and me. How does that sound?"

Consider how the apostle Paul opened his heart to the church at Corinth:

> We do not want you to be unaware, brothers, of the affliction we experienced in Asia. For we were so utterly burdened beyond our strength that we despaired of life itself. Indeed, we felt that we had received the sentence of death. But that was to make us rely not on ourselves but on God who raises the dead. He delivered us from such a deadly peril, and he will deliver us. On him we have set our hope that he will deliver us again. You also must help us by prayer, so that many will give thanks on our behalf for the blessing granted us through the prayers of many.
>
> 2 CORINTHIANS 1:8-11

There's nothing more honest I can do as a dad than be vulnerable with my kids. It might not always feel good or get the response I'm looking for, but my kids know their father is willing to share his heart with them. It's something I need to do even more often, and maybe you do too.

Value: Be Appreciative!

This section isn't about boosting anyone's ego. It's about cherishing the value, dignity, and worth of your Gen Z children. Kids often feel like they *must do good things* in order to receive approval from their parents, but a great way to combat that misconception is by demonstrating that you value and appreciate your Gen Z children simply for who they are, not for what they do for you. This encourages them and gives them a sense of security.

Truth be told, I haven't always valued or acknowledged my kids the way I should. I remember a time on one of our family vacations when I got quite upset with them. We were on our way to dinner to celebrate Mother's Day, and my wife pointed out a beautiful spot near a lagoon, complete with blooming flowers and giant oak trees covered with Spanish moss.

"Let's pull off and take a few family photos right over there," Celia said with excitement.

All four kids in the back seat started to fuss about stopping to take pictures. Of all days, they were complaining about taking family photos with their mom on Mother's Day! We got out of the SUV and walked over to the spot.

"Oh, this is a great location," Celia said. "Don't you think?"

"Yeah, I think it will work. We can put the kids over here where the lighting is perfect," I said, trying to show off my years of watching YouTube videos about photography.

The setting was beautiful, and the light was ideal. There was just one problem—a big problem. None of our kids were smiling. They were more concerned with thoughts of food than of their mother.

Celia was getting irritated, which in turn made me upset.

"You know what, guys?" I said. "You're all acting like spoiled brats! Your mom wants to take family photos with her kids—on Mother's Day, mind you. And none of you are cooperating. Do you expect to get dessert after behaving like this?"

Never before had I told my kids they were spoiled brats. I said those words in frustration, but I didn't believe them. My kids aren't spoiled brats. Are they selfish sometimes? Sure. Have they even been ungrateful? Yeah. But they're not spoiled brats.

Instead of encouraging my family to cooperate, I spoke to my children in a way that didn't value them. Yes, my kids had irritated their mother, but what I said and *how* I said it managed to deflate my entire family all at once.

As we walked back to the SUV, my wife encouraged me to make things right. She asked, "Do you really believe our kids are spoiled brats?"

"No," I immediately replied, the shame evident in my voice. "I was wrong, and I never should have said that. I'm sorry for making things worse."

Standing outside the car with my four kids staring at me in silence made me feel even worse about myself. I could see that I'd hurt them. It was time to clear the air.

"What I said earlier about you guys being spoiled brats was wrong of me," I said. "I shouldn't have said that. I don't want you guys to believe for a second that's what I honestly think of my kids. I value each one of you, and I'm asking you to forgive me for getting upset and saying something hurtful."

At first there was silence from all four of them. Then my oldest son, Tyler, walked over to me. He hugged me and said he forgave me.

The rest of my kids followed suit, and we all embraced as a family.

(Despite the drama, we did manage to get some good photos.)

I like to think I've learned that kids *want* to be noticed, and not just when they're in trouble. In fact, they want you to notice them *especially* when they haven't done anything wrong. They need to know what they mean to you. They need to know they add significance to your life. In short, your kids need you to value them.

Fathers, this is an especially important reminder for you, because it can seem (at times) like our careers and even our possessions are more important than our kids. So, Dad, when you communicate to your children that you treasure them far more than any possession, and that being their father is a label you wear proudly, you will succeed in making your kids feel extra special.

Encourage: Be Supportive!

Coaches need to encourage their players. Teachers need to encourage their students. And parents, of course, need to encourage their children.

Just how important is it for parents to encourage their kids? Let me put it this way: It's life-changing!

Here's a sad fact: In my years of counseling and ministering to teens and young adults, I've discovered that those who receive very little attention or acceptance from their parents are more likely to suffer from isolation, anxiety, and depression.

I recently watched a four-part docuseries about the Unabomber. It attempted to piece together how an intellectual genius like Ted Kaczynski became a cold-blooded killer. In the last episode, some shocking information is revealed as Kaczynski's attorneys prepare to argue for an insanity defense. Kaczynski's attorneys discovered that after entering Harvard University as an academic prodigy at age sixteen, their client was recruited to participate in a multi-year psychological study. Unbeknownst to Kaczynski, the research subjected the participants to psychological abuse and humiliation and tracked any changes in their mental and behavioral habits. I'm certainly not holding these experiments completely responsible for transforming Kaczynski into the Unabomber, but I am asserting that God has hardwired children to both want and need a healthy dose of encouragement. This is especially true when they are younger.

Your encouragement methods might look a bit different with a son versus a daughter, depending on his or her personality. Perhaps your daughter is more of a people pleaser, while your son tends to seek your approval based on his accomplishments. Whether your child is studying for a test, making dinner for the family, trying to fix something, or simply helping around the house, notice these things and look for ways to come alongside and offer encouragement. Proverbs 16:24 tells us, "Gracious words are like a honeycomb, sweetness to the soul and health to the body."

Allow me to illustrate with another example from the Jimenez family. I remember when my two youngest had soccer games on the same day. My son Jackson woke up feeling moody and struggled to get his head in the game. By contrast, his sister Hailey was raring to go from the moment she woke up. Jackson didn't play so well that day, but he did show heart for his teammates by encouraging them during the game. Hailey, meanwhile, played great defense and even had a few shots on goal.

After the games were over, my wife and I encouraged both of our children about their performances, though our approach looked different for each of them. We told Jackson how much we loved watching him support his teammates, but we also encouraged him to have a better attitude and to work on his soccer skills during the week. We applauded Hailey for her tenacity and offered a few suggestions on how she might better engage with her teammates.

With both of our kids, we made sure to praise their strengths rather than focus on their weaknesses. We wanted to encourage, not discourage, them.

Consider your methods of encouragement for each of your kids. Extroverted kids often respond best to verbal affirmation and acceptance, so words of praise are typically a great source of motivation. Introverted kids, however, often prefer affirmation and acceptance delivered in a different way. They need more than just "Great job" or "I'm proud of you." Introverts tend to put greater value on the time you spend with them. You, as the parent, know what motivates your children, and sometimes the best way to offer encouragement is to notice the little things.

Now that you know more about the Jimenez family's *LOVE* concept, feel free to make use of it with your children. We'd be honored to know that other families are benefitting from what God has used to help bless our family. Or perhaps you'd rather come up with your own motto or mission statement. That's great too! Whatever you decide, I assure you: If you start focusing on more laughter, openness, value, and encouragement in your home, it will help strengthen your family's foundation. And you might all have more fun in the process!

Parenting Practice

1. Work on formulating a motto or mission statement that highlights the values you want your family to exhibit. If you're not sure where to start, I suggest using Ephesians 5 as a blueprint.

2. Think of ways you can be more open with your kids. Ask yourself, *Have I shared my testimony with my family? Do I talk to them about my past failures or relationships? When was the last time I opened up to them and shared how God has given me strength?*

3. List all the members of your family and write down exactly why you value each of them. Brainstorm ways that you might express this to them.

4. Consider your kids' different personalities and how they each respond to encouragement. Make a commitment to express some form of encouragement to your kids every day.

9

DISCIPLINE IN THE HOME

IT SEEMS LIKE THE POPULAR THING to do today is to coddle kids, insulate them from conflict, and solve their problems for them. But parents were not put on the earth to please their kids. For you to effectively raise your Gen Z children and keep them anchored in the faith, you will need to exercise the parental authority that the Lord has given you.

Do you recall some of the most popular insurance company slogans?

- "You're in good hands." (Allstate)
- "We keep our promises to you." (Amica)
- "A business of caring." (Cigna)
- "Our plans are based on yours." (Assurant)

How about wireless network campaigns?

- "Stick together." (T-Mobile)
- "We never stop working for you." (Verizon)
- "Mobilizing your world." (AT&T)

Do you see a recurring theme? Each one emphasizes taking care of customers by providing them with the best and most reliable service.

That's the same kind of service that God wants you to give your family.

So take a moment and answer each one of these questions:

- Are your kids in good hands?
- Do you keep your promises to your family?
- Do you spend valuable time with your kids?
- Are you a reliable parent who provides structure and discipline?

I've said this before, and I'll repeat it: Parents are the most powerful and influential people in their child's life. God has given mothers and fathers authority over their kids so that they can raise their kids according to the "discipline and instruction of the Lord" (Ephesians 6:4). That's the way God intended it to be.

But there's still a lot of confusion and even fear regarding how to discipline kids properly. In chapter 3, we examined three common forms of flawed parenting among those currently raising Gen Z. If you recall, I asked you to identify the one form that you struggle with the most.

CONTROL PARENTING	PARANOID PARENTING	DETACHED PARENTING
Failure to Prepare	Failure to Release	Failure to Provide
Oppressive	Obsessive	Oblivious
Wired to Interfere	Controlled by Fear	Geared to Ignore
Creates Conflict	Avoids Conflict	Disregards Conflict

In this chapter, we'll examine four strategies for properly disciplining your kids. The first strategy involves teaching respect for authority and learning how to exercise your authority in the right way. The second strategy is discovering how to best correct your children according to their personalities and temperaments. The third strategy has to do with providing some space for your children to express their opposition. The fourth and final strategy provides guidance on how to implement appropriate consequences so that your children can learn and mature from their mistakes.

FOUR STRATEGIES

The First Strategy: Exercising Authority

One of the most essential life lessons for any parent to teach Gen Zers is respect for authority. Parents need to exercise their authority in the home. I repeat: Parents, *you* are the leaders in your home, not your kids.

Every child has distinctive gifts and blinders and has different ways of expressing emotion. Some children will test boundaries more than others. But how you parent your kids—individually and collectively—will determine how they develop into adulthood.

In his classic parenting book *Shepherding a Child's Heart*, Dr. Tedd Tripp writes, "As a parent, you must exercise authority. You must require obedience of your children because they are called by God to obey and honor you. You must exercise authority, not as a cruel taskmaster, but as one who truly loves them."[1]

Did you catch that? We are never to use our authority to dominate our kids. Instead, as Dr. Tripp rightly points out, we exercise our parental authority over our kids because we love them. When you discipline your child with grace and as God intended, it provides shelter and structure for their lives. They are less likely to disobey you and more likely to obey you.

It's crucial to have a correct view of your authority when disciplining your children. But before we address that view, let me bring up two common parenting mistakes that can diminish your authority in the home. They are (1) giving in to the demands of your children and (2) bribing them for favors. I've been a part of parenting classes wherein moms and dads admit that giving in and bribing their kids isn't right, but those very same parents make excuses for why they still do it.

Let's look at why giving in to your child's demands or bribing your child isn't good for you or them.

We'll start with giving in. When you give in to a child's demands, you're essentially giving up your authority. In other words, your child's demands override your commands. The same logic applies to bribing your kids. Every time you "pay off" your children to get them to listen or obey, you "sell off" a bit more of your control as the parent. This path will eventually render you powerless, unable to lead your home and unable to properly correct your children.

Here are a few examples of what *not* to do or say:

- "If you take out the recycling, I'll let you stay up to watch another show."
- "If you look after your sister, I'll let you go out with your friends this weekend."
- "Tell me what you want so that I can get you to listen to me."

Giving in to your kids promotes disobedience, and bribery incentivizes selfishness. Proverbs 15:27 tells us, "Whoever is greedy for unjust gain troubles his own household, but he who hates bribes will live."

In the chart below, the left column shows the negative results of giving in and bribery. The right column lists the benefits of properly exercising your authority as a parent.

GIVING IN AND BRIBING	LEADING AND NEGOTIATING
Losing the Moral High Ground	Establishing Ground Rules
Forfeiting Respect	Achieving Respect
Making Things Worse	Working Things Out

It's never easy for parents who are trapped in a negative cycle to break those habits. Many parents ask me how to regain their authority in the home. My response is always the same: You have to take responsibility for what you've done (or haven't done) in the past, change your current mentality toward parenting, and commit to God's blueprint for raising kids, which includes exercising your authority as a parent. Yes, you will likely experience pushback from your kids, but your children won't be barking orders at you if you're the one leading them.

The Second Strategy: Correcting Your Children

Teaching my four kids how to ride a bike was considerably different each time. They learned at different ages and in their own distinct ways. With Tyler, we went outside after dinner one evening to just get the basics down. He was cautious, did everything by the book, and was riding by himself the next day. Amy, on the other hand, took several days to get the hang of it. It got to the point where her mom had to step in to help complete the training. Jackson was nervous right from the start. His main issue was trying to stay balanced on his bike, since he typically fell after going a few yards. It took a good week and several sessions to make sure Jackson was ready to ride on his own. Finally, there was Hailey, our youngest. Before I even made it outside to help her, she was attempting to ride her bike all by herself. That crazy girl!

I share this bike-riding illustration to point out the necessity of understanding how each of your children tick and the best way to adapt to their individual temperaments so that your instruction or correction will be more effective (see Proverbs 3:1-2).

Sadly, some parents today shy away from correcting their kids for fear of being seen as authoritarian or somehow upsetting their children. For many parents, trying to get their kids to obey—or even just pay attention—is like pulling teeth. But as I said earlier, parents need to exercise their authority if they hope to discipline their children effectively. Proverbs 13:24 says, "Whoever spares the rod hates his son, but he who loves him is diligent to discipline him."

To be clear, when the Bible talks about disciplining your child, it doesn't necessarily refer to punishment. Discipline in the Bible mainly has to do with instructing, protecting, teaching, and guiding your child. I like how my colleague Danny Huerta describes the discipline referenced in Proverbs 13:24: "Part of discipline is establishing boundaries, and boundaries are comforting for everyone. They're especially comforting to children who are trying to figure out the world and testing limits and authority. It's helpful to think of your parenting role as that of a shepherd, guiding your children's paths and protecting them."[2]

Throughout Proverbs, we are told that discipline imparts wisdom to your child (Proverbs 29:15), deters your child from reckless living and possible harm (Proverbs 23:14), and even promotes peace in your family (Proverbs 29:17, NIV). When you discipline your child, you are exercising your God-given authority and loving your child by modeling God's correction (Proverbs 3:11-12). And when you do correct your child, you are helping to build character.

But when you avoid or neglect correcting your child, it will only perpetuate an atmosphere of disrespect. The more you enable disrespectful behavior, the worse off your home life will be.

In some of my parenting classes, I use the principles below. I came up with them as a simple way to help my audience see how their actions (or lack thereof) as parents can lead to either a positive or a negative response from their children.

LACK OF CORRECTION = LACK OF RESPECT

RESPECT THROUGH CORRECTION = RESPECTFUL RESPONSES

To help illustrate the principles above, let me introduce you to David and Terry. They've been married for nearly fifteen years and have two kids. They represent the first principle: *lack of correction = lack of respect.* David's style of parenting is, well, nonexistent. Whenever his children get upset or raise their voices, David shuts down. He's even been known to exit the room, leaving his wife to deal with the emotional chaos alone. Terry, as you can surely imagine, is fed up with David's abdication of his parental authority. She's not sure how much more she can take—whether of the children's constant disrespect or of David's refusal to get involved.

What we have with David and Terry is a classic case of *enabling* their kids' rebellious behavior. Instead of confronting poor attitudes and teaching their children to behave better, these parents have allowed their kids to continue in their disrespect. This is because neither David nor Terry likes conflict and neither one wants to be the parental version of the "bad cop." This has inevitably led to a lack of respect in the home.

It is up to you, Mom *and* Dad, to keep the peace. It's up to you to work together. If you don't work as a team, then the atmosphere at home will deteriorate.

Now let's move on to a more pleasant family situation.

Will and Emily have been married for more than twenty years, and they have five kids. They represent the second principle: *respect through correction = respectful responses.*

Because Will and Emily respect and embrace their roles as father and mother, they, in turn, are united in their parenting. Anytime a situation arises where one of their five kids crosses the line, Will and Emily respond in love by consistently correcting that child. This causes their children to respond in obedience because they respect their parents and trust that they know what's best for the family.

In the case of Will and Emily, several things stand out: First, they are firm believers that *respect*, not rules, strengthens relationships. Second—and along those same lines—they don't create arbitrary boundaries as a way to control or manipulate their children. The limits they've established are for their children's security, comfort, and protection—and for them to learn restraint. Third, when their kids do cross the line, Will and Emily are there to *correct* (not punish) their children and teach them valuable lessons. Fourth, Will and Emily are the kind of parents who know when their children are behaving *defiantly* versus simply being *childish*. Thus, they know when to correct a behavior and when to let their kids be kids (see Proverbs 22:15). Finally, no matter how upsetting the situation, Will and Emily remain accountable to God and each other to avoid losing their cool.

That's what it looks like to parent with wisdom and grace.

Before we transition into the third strategy, I'd like you to consider a few questions:

- Who is your most challenging child and why?
- How do you speak to and/or treat that child?
- Do you typically have to raise your voice to get him or her to listen?
- How do you handle that child when he or she isn't listening?

A word of encouragement: The conflicts you likely face with your strongest-willed child aren't because you somehow love him or her less than the others. Most families have at least one strong-willed child, and that child—as you're well aware, and you likely have the scars to prove it—knows just how to push your buttons. Moving forward, a great passage to help guide you when dealing with this particular child is 1 Corinthians 13:4-7, which says, "Love is patient and kind; love does not envy or boast; it is not arrogant or rude. It does not insist on its own way; it is not irritable or resentful; it does not rejoice at wrongdoing, but rejoices with the truth. Love bears all things, believes all things, hopes all things, endures all things."

The Third Strategy: Allowing Some Protest

If you have a tween or teen in your home, they will inevitably protest a rule or let you know about a boundary they don't like. When this happens, don't immediately dismiss them. It is only natural for kids to express their opinions or start to push back as they get older. They may not always be correct, but they're not always and automatically wrong. This will vary depending on what stage of parenting you're in.

If you want to spare yourself many unhelpful arguments, I believe it's essential that you and your spouse (if you're married) agree to let your older children express their disagreements without interruption. That said, your children also need to be respectful when communicating their grievances. If they can do that, then let them know that you are willing to hear them out. Listening to your kids voice their concerns conveys that you care about them and respect their growing maturity. It will probably require added patience on your part, but when you take the time to listen to your children, it will inevitably strengthen the bond between you.[3]

This doesn't mean that you will frequently give in to their protests. It simply means that you'll hear your children out.

Here are a few questions to ask yourself as you listen to your child's perspective:

- *Is his or her request reasonable?*
- *Why is my son making such a big deal of this?*
- *What is it that my daughter truly wants from me?*
- *When was the last time I allowed my daughter to do something she felt old enough to do?*
- *Does my son believe that I trust him?*
- *What will happen if I agree to what my child wants?*

After listening to your child's protest, let it sink in for a minute. Don't issue a hasty decision, and please don't simply pull rank and shut down your child's request. I remind parents that there's a delicate balance between *validation* and *correction*. We need to make sure we validate our child's feelings and viewpoints before implementing a plan of correction. A great counselor friend once told me, "Parents tend to spend more time lecturing than they do inquiring."

So instead of telling your child what's *going* to happen, look at him or her and say, "I appreciate you expressing to me how you feel. I didn't realize you felt this way about _____. I want you to know that I love you and want nothing more than to work this out together."

When you respond this way, it will do three things: (1) Ideally, it will help defuse your child's frustrations; (2) it will help affirm your child; and (3) it will remind your child that you are not enemies. You certainly might disagree, and your child might still believe that your rules aren't fair. But regardless of your decision or where the two of you stand on the issue, the main thing is that you will always love each other.

After you listen and communicate your desire to work together, you still might need additional information. This is your time to ask questions in response to your child's challenge. I want to point out that this exchange is not a cross-examination. So any lawyers reading this—or apologists, like me—please keep that in mind.

A few simple questions to consider asking your child include the following:

- "Whatever my decision is, do you believe it's motivated by my love for you?"
- "How would you feel if I said *no* to your request?"
- "How would you feel if my decision was *yes*?"
- "Is there something I've done to cause you to feel this way?"

The first stage of this hypothetical conversation is when your child *expresses what he or she wants to happen*. (In other words, the reason for the protest.) The second stage involves seriously *contemplating that protest and asking questions* to see how your child is thinking through his or her feelings. Posing additional questions to your child gives both of you the opportunity to consider how the issue can or should be resolved.

The third and final stage of this process is to *seek a resolution*. You might determine that your existing rule or boundary must stand, and you certainly have that right (and sometimes that responsibility) as the parent. Then again, you might seek a resolution in the form of a compromise—some middle ground between your original position and your child's wishes. And maybe, just maybe, your son or daughter is right. Perhaps it *is* time to let go and give them more freedom in determining what they think is best. Whatever you decide, try to make sure that your decision is in keeping with the integrity of the request, the state of your relationship, and your son's or daughter's level of respect when presenting the request.

The Fourth Strategy: Implementing Appropriate Consequences

Engage your imagination for a moment and picture yourself attempting to disarm a bomb. That probably sounds pretty dramatic and far-fetched, so if you're having trouble, just try to think of a movie or television show with a scene involving a bomb.

While most of you won't be disarming bombs anytime soon, there are probably other kinds of explosives lurking in your home. Perhaps you have a kid with a short fuse, ready to blow at any minute. Some parents would find disarming a bomb less intimidating and complicated than confronting a child who is about to explode.

Much like Will and Emily, the couple we met earlier, you also have to respond to behavioral problems with your kids and deal with difficult situations. When things get messy, uncomfortable, and sometimes ugly, that's when you must step in to calm the situation. It's not much fun, but getting involved shows the entire family—especially your children—that they matter. They matter so much that you are willing to get in the mud with them.

That's where consequences for inappropriate behavior come in. They're absolutely necessary, but many parents raising Gen Z are fickle when it comes to dishing out consequences. What happens the first time your children disobey you? The second time? Are there any consequences if your kids talk back to you? Or if you catch them in a lie? What happens if you find your teen texting friends in the middle of the night—after you told them to go to bed?

When it comes to carrying out consequences, I want to help you avoid issuing ineffective ones by introducing three principles designed to elevate your discipline at home.

When I was a young dad, my approach to carrying out consequences was, at times, misguided and implemented with the wrong intentions. I now refer to my former approach as "scattered consequences"—I would dish out random, reactionary consequences. In other words, I rarely gave my actions any thought. And that approach didn't change until I had a conversation with an older gentleman whom I greatly admire. He graciously shared with me some parenting tips that helped transform both my family and me.

Since that conversation, I've tinkered a bit with my friend's advice and developed three principles to help clear up my own misguidedness and bring clarity to how I carry out consequences with my kids. I'll share them with you in the hope that they will bring you the same clarity.

1. CONSEQUENCES ARE A TEACHING LESSON

Dealing with a child's rebellion is a time-sensitive issue that requires your presence, your attention, and (usually) a prompt response. I'm not suggesting that discipline should always be implemented immediately; there are times when your child's poor choices will come with consequences of their own. Sometimes the feelings they experience after being disobedient or irresponsible are all the consequences your son or daughter needs to learn a lesson. Occasionally you need to adopt a laissez-faire approach, especially with older Gen Zers.

In *The Christian Parenting Handbook*, authors Scott Turansky and Joanne Miller remind parents of the aim of correction: "Remember that the goal is a changed heart, not just punishment for doing wrong."[4] Turansky and Miller bring up a critical point: If we're being honest with ourselves, many parents tend to focus on the *wrong* our child committed but not on how to teach that child a lesson—how to learn from that poor choice.

Other times it will be clear that you need to step in and implement a specific consequence for your child's poor choice. Turansky and Miller explain it this way: "A larger consequence may be needed to get the child's attention, but the real work takes place by helping children adjust the way they think and by training them to develop mature behavior. Often, many small corrections are more effective than one large consequence."[5]

Therefore, when correcting your child, try to make sure that your correction—whenever possible—helps develop your child's maturity and enhances your relationship with them. Do whatever you can to avoid jeopardizing the trust you've established between you and your child.

2. CONSEQUENCES REQUIRE A CALM APPROACH

Whenever you enforce a measure of correction at home, never do so in anger or when you're feeling particularly emotional. Keep your cool and avoid overreacting. Proverbs 29:11 says, "A fool always loses his temper, but a wise person holds it back" (NASB).

In the chart below, notice the difference between overreacting (on the left) and responding in love (on the right).

Repairing the Damage

- Guilt, regret, and fear
- Anger and impatience
- Unreasonable expectations
- Jumping to conclusions

- Understanding
- Patience
- Reasonable expectations
- Resolving the issues

Parents often make the mistake of assuming that our kids did something wrong without verifying it first. That is due (in large part) to letting anger and impatience get the best of us. If this has happened to you and you want to repair the damage and help heal your child's heart, then you need to approach the situation with the right attitude. A great prayer to say before implementing consequences comes from Psalm 51:10: "Create in me a clean heart, O God, and renew a right spirit within me."

In order to maintain a calm approach and avoid overreacting, here are a few sample phrases to say to your child:

- "Can you help me understand why you ignored what you were told?"
- "I realize you don't like my decision, and that's okay—I don't expect you to. But I do expect you to understand that I am making the decisions I believe are best for you and for our family."
- "I want you to know that I love you, but the way you acted is unacceptable, and I cannot allow you to behave this way."
- "I might be upset that you didn't do what I told you, but that doesn't mean I am mad at you."

3. CONSEQUENCES INVOLVE A MEASURED OUTCOME

Make sure that the punishment fits the crime. For example, let's say your son accidently scratches your car. Do you ban him from driving your car for life? Well, maybe if it's a Bentley or Maserati.

(I'm just kidding!) Of course you don't; it was an accident. Or how about if your daughter breaks her curfew and neglects to call or text you? Do you take away *all* her privileges for six months, or do you take away *some* privileges for a while? Well, that depends. Did she simply lose track of time, or did she intentionally undermine your authority? Was she at a friend's house—someone you approve of—watching a movie, or was she out drinking with friends you disapprove of? The answers to these questions absolutely matter because they will help determine the punishment that best fits the crime.

The purpose of implementing consequences is to teach your children valuable lessons. Follow the counsel of Proverbs 19:18, which reads, "Discipline your son, for there is hope; do not set your heart on putting him to death." In other words, keep your anger or resentment from leading you to impose inappropriate punishments on your children.

The loss of rewards or privileges isn't the main concern for you as the parent. Your primary concern is your children's response to discipline. If they take responsibility and accept the consequences, then there's always the option for you to reduce those restrictions. If and when you choose to do so, it can be an excellent lesson in redemption. Proverbs 13:1 tells us, "A wise son heeds *and* accepts [and is the result of] his father's discipline *and* instruction, But a scoffer does not listen to reprimand *and* does not learn from his errors" (AMP).

My hope is that you will take the four strategies for parental discipline listed and discussed in this chapter and apply them consistently and faithfully in your home. No matter what happens, stick to your guns and follow through with the appropriate consequences. It is my prayer that your loving approach to discipline will win the hearts of your children as you help them draw close to God.

Parenting Practice

1. As a parent, you want to move from *avoidance* to *acceptance* in implementing consequences. Instead of simply avoiding a situation or a conflict, you must accept your role as parent and step in to address the problem. You need to embrace your position and be the authority in your home. This will inspire your children to do the same someday.

2. The boundaries you set for your children need to be based on specific, consistent standards. Your children's behavior will almost certainly test those limits, and you should revisit those limits when necessary, such as when they get older and exhibit more maturity. Limits can be adjusted, but your standards cannot.

3. Avoid giving in to aggression or manipulation, whether it originates with you or your children.

4. Be careful of the tone you use with your kids. Girls sometimes respond better to a gentler tone combined with more explanation. Boys, on the other hand, often react better to a firmer tone with an emphasis on appreciation. Every child is different, of course, so be prepared to adjust your approach as necessary.

5. Danny Huerta, vice president of parenting and youth at Focus on the Family, has written a fantastic book called *7 Traits of Effective Parenting*.[6] I encourage you and your spouse to read it in conjunction with this book.

10

THREE ADJUSTMENTS YOU (ALMOST CERTAINLY) NEED TO MAKE

HOW OFTEN DO YOU HEAR SOMEONE say that they have too much time on their hands? In reality, it's usually the opposite—most of us are so busy that by day's end we're too tired to do much of anything. Simply put, this has got to stop. It's affecting not only our health but also our relationships with our kids.

There was a time, back when my kids were younger, when I was seriously annoyed by their little hands banging on my office door, wanting to come in. I can't tell you how many times I'd enter my office to find Amy pretending to type on my computer or Jackson spinning around and around in my office chair. I think back to when Hailey would come barging in to show me her latest drawing of Elsa from the movie *Frozen* or when Tyler was barely waist-high, begging me to take a break so the two of us could go out for a burger.

Boy, things have changed *a lot* since then. I wonder now what I was thinking! Those "annoying" interruptions were my precious kids wanting to spend time with me—their daddy. Now that my oldest two have left the nest and the other two are entering their teen years, I treasure every single one of those "interruptions." I now find myself soaking up whatever time I can get with all four of them.

What about you, Mom and Dad? Do you resent similar opportunities with your kids, or are you investing time in each one of your children? (For those of you who are divorced and share custody of your kids, I'm sure that it's extra hard to manage your time with them!)

Whatever your home life looks like, I want to help you be wise with your time so you can invest more of it where it counts the most—with your children.

It seemed like things were a lot simpler back when my parents were raising my brothers and me. There were fewer distractions (I think), and my parents didn't seem to feel any pressure to fill our days with so many activities. Back then, of course, we didn't have the same number of commitments competing for our time that Gen Z has today.

Raising Gen Zers in today's fast-paced culture is like playing tug-of-war. Many parents constantly lament how little time they enjoy together. Every member of the family, it seems, has places to be and pressing matters that need attention. When you take stock of all the demands and self-imposed commitments, you typically find that parents (just like you) are, quite frankly, overwhelmed with everything.

If that's you, then pause, take a deep breath, and pray. Once you're in the right frame of mind, spend some time reflecting on each of the questions below:

- *How much time do I spend with my children each day?*
- *Am I so busy and unavailable that my kids feel unimportant?*

- *What does the family usually end up doing when everyone is at home?*
- *How many days each week do we typically eat dinner together as a family?*

I don't know the specifics of your busy life, but one thing I do know is that many parents want to make more time for family and build lasting memories. The adjustments below are designed to help you maximize your time with your kids and turn that time into memorable moments. But I must warn you ahead of time (no pun intended) that each adjustment will require developing new habits. You'll need to confront some not-so-good behaviors that you're willing to change. If that's something you think you can do, then let's get to it![1]

THE FIRST ADJUSTMENT: BE MINDFUL

Have you ever noticed how you can be physically present with your kids but not there mentally?

In a five-year survey on overloaded lives, Professor Michael Zigarelli described the trickle-down effect that the busyness of life has on families: "It may be the case that 1) Christians are assimilating to a culture of busyness, hurry and overload, which leads to 2) God becoming more marginalized in Christians' lives, which leads to 3) a deteriorating relationship with God, which leads to 4) Christians becoming even more vulnerable to adopting secular assumptions about how to live, which leads to 5) more conformity to a culture of busyness, hurry and overload. And then the cycle begins again."[2]

In his book *The Ruthless Elimination of Hurry*, Pastor John Mark Comer refers to the "culture of busyness" as "distracting ourselves into spiritual oblivion."[3] When the daily grind of our busy schedules causes us to lose focus on what really matters—God and family—that's when we know we have a problem. Your kids can tell when you're not mindful of the things of God or of what's going on in their lives.

— — —

Growing up, I loved to play basketball. That's all I wanted to do. My mom, on the other hand, didn't care for basketball. She disliked sports in general. When my dad, brothers, and I would watch hoops on TV, my mother was never in sight. More often than not, she was either reading a book or tidying the house.

But when it came to *my* basketball games, my mom was always there—sitting in the stands and enthusiastically cheering for her son. It was embarrassing at times, I'll admit, but her presence left a deep and lasting impression on me. Why? Because although my mom was generally clueless about sports, she was clued in to her son's passion for basketball. And that was reason enough for her to make time to share that passion with me.

What about you, Mom and Dad? What is preventing you from making the time you spend with your kids more of a priority? Take, for example, the diagram below. Each of the four sections represents a habit that may take up part of your day, thereby making you unavailable for more time with your family. Which habit would you say most applies to you?

being on my phone a lot	binge-watching shows
"escaping" to my bedroom	avoiding outside activities

Now take your primary habit and match it with the corresponding response in the diagram below. For example, if you're on your phone a lot, a simple (though not always easy) adjustment is to put it away.

put away the phone	turn off the TV
play a family game	do an outside activity

Your habit might not seem like much of a problem. But trust me, there's a good chance that it is.

By making a few simple adjustments, you'll likely be surprised by how many "bonus hours" you can carve out in a given week. Over time, you should start to see an improvement in your own family mindfulness—how you interact and spend time with your kids.

This is the big question: *Do you see the need and have the desire to make these adjustments?* More to the point: *Will you make a conscious effort to unplug from your work and your gadgets in order to connect more with your family?*

When I get sucked into gadgets and projects, I remind myself of seven benefits that result when I am consciously present with my kids. I hope these reminders will empower you as they do me:

1. Time with my kids makes them feel loved and cherished.
2. Time with my kids helps them develop coping skills.
3. Time with my kids helps reduce their stress and frustration.
4. Time with my kids fosters a positive self-image.
5. Time with my kids helps boost their confidence.
6. Time with my kids motivates them to be respectful, open, and honest.
7. Time with my kids enriches our relationships.

I've stated this obvious fact before, but it bears repeating: Parents are not perfect. We *will* make poor decisions sometimes, and there will be plenty of times when we don't give our children the attention they need and deserve. We are only human, after all, but we shouldn't let that keep us from striving to make changes for the better.

As the chart below illustrates, you can begin this process by making just one minor change in your life and sticking to it. Once that change becomes a habit, then make another change or adjustment. It's important to remember that your end goal is to be more intentional about carving out time for your kids.

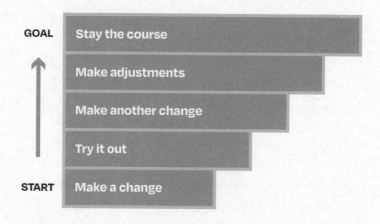

At first it won't be easy. It will require effort and sacrifice. There will be things you'll need to give up to make more time for your family. You might not like it right away, but if it means more time with your kids, then you owe it to them—and *you*—to make that change!

THE SECOND ADJUSTMENT: SLOW DOWN

As I mentioned in chapter 4, Gen Z is exhausted, and they are experiencing higher-than-usual levels of stress and depression—much of which they are unable to handle alone. Yet Gen Zers are not the only ones feeling overwhelmed. An increasing number of parents are voicing their concerns about and seeking solutions to their own busy lives. Check out the blatant honesty of how this Canadian mom felt after signing up her kids for more and more activities:

> I'm going to be up front here, even though what I'm about
> to say may dishearten some of you: I hate kids' activities.
> I'll explain. I hate the stress of being online at 6:58 a.m.
> and refreshing the page until 7 a.m. to score $206 per kid
> swimming lessons on Sunday mornings. (I also hate how
> expensive activities are.) I hate the politics. I hate how
> parents berate their kids when they don't hit the ball; I
> hate how parents stare at their phones instead of watching
> their kids at bat. I'm not a fan of extracurriculars outside
> of school-run activities, but I think they're important for
> all the reasons you probably do. But how do parents know
> if their brood are committed to too many after-school and
> weekend undertakings?[4]

I'm sure most of you can relate to this mom, but here's the thing: Do you simply keep complaining about how chaotic your schedule is, or are you doing something to change it? For instance, what do you do when one kid wants to play basketball, another wants to join the swim team, and your third child's friend is begging her to sign up for band practice after school? Do you just find a way to cram it into your already-busy schedule?

Parents think that more classes, more tutoring, and more extracurricular activities will automatically make our kids smarter and better prepared for the real world. But that's just not the case. More busyness in no way means that your children will be ready for what awaits them in life.

This brings us to the logical adjustment: *Slow down.*

As the parent, it's up to you to set the speed limits in your family. If your family is racing through life, it's your job to apply the brakes. Slowing things down may be challenging, especially considering all the stuff you probably have going on right now. But there are many benefits to running the race at a slightly slower pace. Those benefits include more serenity and relaxation. Improved health. Less stress. More downtime with the family. Isn't that what we're all looking for?

My wife and I have learned that it takes effort to make time for family in between my traveling and speaking engagements. It's not always easy, but we try to not let the busyness of life interfere with our family time or drive a wedge between us. After all, there is always *something* to compete with my time at home. Another meeting to attend. Another conference to speak at. Another book or article to write. At some point, however, I need to consider my limitations (along with my family's) and say, "Sorry, but I can't add another thing to my schedule." That's what it means to slow down. It's about learning to say *no.*

Your best way forward is to sit down as a family and create a master calendar. After taking into account time for sleep, school, work, homework, and dinner with family, you may be left with a couple of hours to work with each day. Maybe.

To help determine which extracurricular activities should remain on the calendar, follow the five criteria below:

- It needs to be something my child really loves to do.
- It needs to fit within the family budget.
- It needs to work with the family schedule.
- It needs to help develop my child's physical, emotional, or social skills.

- It needs to be something my child is willing to take ownership of. (In other words, if you need to motivate your child to participate, then it becomes *your* problem.)

THE THIRD ADJUSTMENT: SAVOR THE MOMENTS

As I'm writing this, I'm aware of three families who have experienced great sadness.

The first family recently lost their father to cancer. He is survived by a wife and five children. My wife and I had the chance to sit with that man—my friend—before he passed away. I will never forget the feeling I had that day when I saw what cancer had done to my friend. His skin was yellowed, and random patches of hair dotted his head. His body was so frail that he was almost unrecognizable.

The second family is a couple who endured what no parents want to face—the loss of a child. My wife and I would sometimes visit their CaringBridge website to see how the family was doing. We would see their son's pictures and read the sweet stories that his mother and father shared. It broke our hearts, but it was also very touching to see how devoted this couple was to their son.

The third family's situation hits hardest of all because it is my brother's family. It pains me to write this, but I lost my brother Joe to cancer in 2019. He was only forty-two years old. The bewildering landscape of grief was hard to navigate at times. He, too, left behind a wife and five precious children.

If these families knew years ago what was coming, think about how they would have savored their moments together.

That's what I want to convey to you in this final section of part 3. Don't take for granted the moments you have with your kids. Instead, savor them as though they might be your last. Think of it this way: You know those times when you are so overwhelmed by love for your family that you just want to hug and kiss them? That's what I'm talking about when it comes to savoring your time together.

I'm not saying you need to take your kids out to fancy restaurants or book a vacation at an expensive beach house. I'm talking about savoring those everyday moments with your kids, whether in the car, at the dinner table, when friends come over, or at church. Let's take a closer look at those everyday moments.

Car Rides

If your family is anything like mine, you spend several hours each week in the car. Since I have four kids of various ages, getting them all where they need to be isn't always something I've enjoyed. But one day while driving—yes, I get the irony—I had an epiphany. Or, I should say, a change of heart. The skies didn't open up, and an angel didn't appear to me. All I can say is that I glanced over at my daughter Amy, and it was as if I suddenly saw her as a grown woman. Just like that, I began to savor car rides with my kids.

Today, Amy has a job and drives herself to work. She's even taking college classes. Man, time sure does fly, and I'm glad I learned to treasure that time with my kids, even if we were sometimes stuck in traffic!

Car rides are excellent opportunities to catch up on what's happening with your kids, give them a pep talk before a game, or—one of our favorite things to do—just listen to music together.

Family Meals

Dinnertime is an opportunity to both feed our bellies and feed our souls, and we get to do it as a family. It's a time to wind down, catch up on the day, and hang out together while enjoying good food.

For some families, regular, nightly dinners are not always easy or convenient. And that's okay. Some things are out of our control. But whenever possible, try to work out a few nights a week to dine together. I promise that you won't regret it. Research shows that regular family dinners can enhance your children's cognitive and language skills, improve their mental and physical health, boost their school grades, and reduce the likelihood of them getting involved with drugs or crime.[5]

Hanging Out with Friends

Recently, my two older kids invited several friends over to our house for a cookout and Bible study. My wife and I weren't planning to hang out with a bunch of teenagers in our basement. We were going to help prepare the food and leave the rest to them. But that's not the way it happened.

Before we knew it, we were all talking, playing games, and taking prayer requests late into the evening. I have to say, even though my wife and I didn't get to enjoy the TV show we wanted to watch that night, I can tell you that we still had a lot of fun.

It's good to hang with your kids and their friends sometimes because it gives you a chance to see a different side of them and learn to give them space as they develop relationships outside the home. So when was the last time you spent time with your kids and their friends? What are some ways you can have a positive impact on your older children and their peers? (But be careful to avoid getting in the way and making the group reluctant to speak freely.)

Church Life

Let's admit it, church attendance is no longer a priority for many Christian families because so many other activities take precedence. Every weekend, the vicious cycle of showing up for sporting events, running errands, and simply conserving energy for the week ahead makes it difficult sometimes to work up the motivation for attending church.

Yet regular church attendance and participation in worship services need to be a top priority for Christian families. Going to church and gathering together with friends from church are wonderful opportunities to spend time with your kids.

The church is a place created for families to come and worship our Lord and Savior Jesus Christ, to grow in our faith, and to build community with other like-minded believers. Attending church together regularly is one more reminder that we need to protect our time as a family, to invest in our faith, and to not let other distractions invade that time.

It is my conviction that by being more mindful of how you interact with your kids, by slowing down the busyness of life, and by savoring the moments spent with family, you will begin to see significant differences in your children's lives, and in yours as well.

Parenting Practice

1. Ask the Lord to help you be more mindful about investing in your kids' lives every day.

2. Be proactive about spending time with your children in ways that speak to them and their personalities.

3. Set aside time to disconnect from technology so you can better connect as a family.

4. Sit down to plan some fun things you can all do together.

5. Make sure your kids have several free hours each week in which they can do the things *they* want to do.

6. Find a nonprofit that your family can serve together, whether a few times a year or even once a month.

7. If you have more than one child, make a regular habit of taking each one out for a treat, whether it's a burger or a milkshake—or both! Spend the time together *listening* to how they are doing. Ask about role models, friendships, desires, and faith. Reinforce your love for them and remind them that you are always available to talk and pray.

8. Consider inviting over a family from church at least once a month. If you are not currently involved with a local church, then make finding one your first priority.

PART FOUR

FORGING A PATHWAY FOR
GEN Z

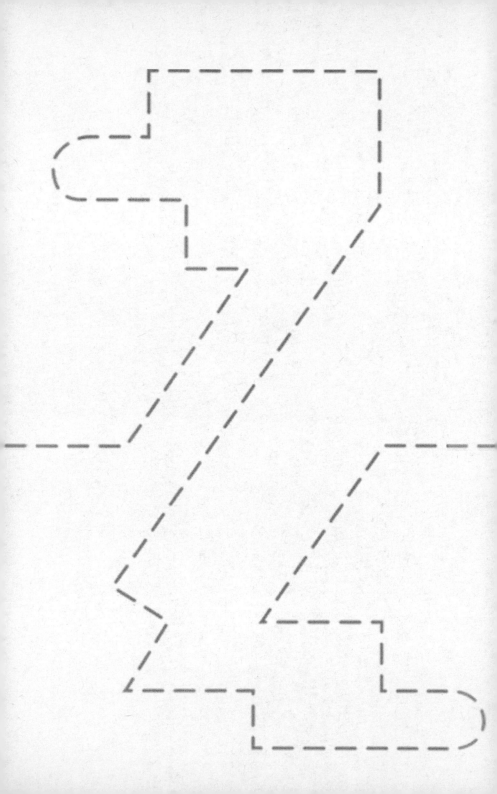

11

MODEL YOUR FAITH AT HOME AND BEYOND

WHENEVER I'M WRITING, I put my cell phone on silent mode or turn it off altogether. Yet one morning I must have forgotten, because my phone dinged while I was deep at work.

My first instinct was to throw the phone across the room, but a sudden urge to look at the text overpowered my agitation. I glanced to see who the text was from, but there was no name—just an unfamiliar number and a message that read:

> **Hey, Jason. Sorry to bother you but I really need to talk. My wife is at it again about me needing to be a better example to our kids. I'm trying but my wife doesn't think I am. Need some counsel. Thanks!**

My first thought was, *Who on earth is this, and why don't I have his number in my contacts?*

Anxious to find out, I texted back what seemed to be a distressed dad:

Hey! So sorry to hear this. Your name isn't coming up. Let me know who you are so I can help you out. Thx!

I waited for a response, but nothing came. Trouble is, I was now *invested*. Trying to figure out who this dad was made it nearly impossible for me to concentrate on my work.

Finally, after what seemed like an hour (probably only five minutes), the dad texted back.

He told me who he was—let's call him Brad—and asked if there was a time we could get together. The name was a blast from the past, and I was surprised to hear about his family problems because this man was a prominent figure in our community.

When I met Brad for lunch, he was reserved at first. Yet I sensed that he was on the verge of a breakdown. He had aged a lot since I'd last seen him. I knew that if I wanted Brad to open up, I would probably need to take the lead. I began to share some of my ups and downs as a husband and a father. I also tried to reassure him that he was not alone in whatever he was going through at home. The entire time I talked, Brad's eyes never drifted from me. He listened intently, barely moving a muscle.

Finally, Brad leaned forward, pushed aside his food, and said, "Wait a second. You struggle too? I mean, come on. You're a pastor and write books on this sort of stuff."

"Yes, Brad. I struggle too," I replied. "We all do. But the Bible declares that God's grace is sufficient for us, and it is God who gives us the power to overcome our struggles and weaknesses."

During the hour or so that we spent together, Brad shared how his own father wasn't there for him growing up. He also said he never had a godly man teach him how to lead his home or grow in his Christian faith. Brad had managed to be quite successful in business, but he admitted he was ignorant about being a spiritual leader to his kids.

Much of what I'm going to cover in this chapter is what I explained to Brad. And by the way, Brad is doing much better now. He's learning to be a spiritual leader and has gotten plugged in with a supportive group of other Christian men.

ESSENTIAL WORKERS

In 2015, a company called MasterClass launched an online educational platform featuring specialized video classes taught by leading experts in their respective fields.

Want to learn how to cook? Look no further; your MasterClass instructor is none other than Gordon Ramsay himself. Or how about taking a filmmaking course taught by legendary directors Martin Scorsese and Ron Howard? Are you an athlete who wants to up your game? You're in luck, because Steph Curry and Serena Williams will be your coaches and teach you everything they've learned about being the best at basketball and tennis.

And the list goes on.

When you think about it, it's remarkable what you can learn in the digital age—in the comfort of your own home. Yet as exciting as this sounds, there are still limits to what digital learning can provide. Most importantly, it cannot offer human contact. Digital tools are largely impersonal, designed primarily for convenience. After all, personal interaction is an essential aspect of the most effective forms of education. If you genuinely want to learn from an expert, it's best to be around them.

What does this have to do with parenting? Everything.

During the COVID-19 quarantines of 2020, doctors and first responders were essential workers who treated patients and imparted medical advice to help get us through the pandemic. Yet your role as parents in your children's lives is just as significant, if not more so, than that of doctors and first responders. God has placed you in your children's lives for a divine purpose. Whether you have one child or a house full of them—you, Mom and Dad, are absolutely *essential* workers whose duty it is to impart God's truth to those in your care.

The day will come when the children you've cared for and nurtured will question whether your faith in Jesus is genuine. At some point in your children's lives, they will have to decide for themselves what to believe and whether to follow what you said and what you taught them.

SIX WAYS TO MODEL YOUR FAITH

As American society grows increasingly secular, Christianity no longer represents the kind of authority and influence it once had with previous generations. Church attendance is no longer a top priority for the bulk of young Americans, and a growing number of Christians don't see the need to put down roots in a local congregation.

Is our faith, then, a lost cause? Do we toss in the towel and admit defeat? Absolutely not. Gen Z is desperate for guidance, for inspiration. Their parents need to model their faith consistently, and with passion and conviction. I get asked this question a lot: "Jason, what's the solution to reaching young people for Christ?"

My answer? You. Parents.

I've put together six proven steps to guide you as you live out your faith in front of your family.

The First Step: Model Your Personal Relationship with Jesus

When you think about it, it's intimidating to realize that your kids are always watching to see how you respond to adversity. No matter what you do, what you say, or how you say it, your behavior will influence your children. So do your best to be a positive example for your kids, even though you might not always model appropriate behavior.

As it turns out, when you take a closer look at the 30 percent of Gen Zers who indicate having a relationship with Jesus, you find that most of their parents are Christians too.

What does that tell you? It means you should never underestimate the power of a parent's influence.

> Only a small percentage of Gen Z look to religious role models to help them shape their lives and mature in their faith.

I'm sure you've heard the saying "Faith is caught, not taught." Well, I hate to break it to you, but that statement isn't true. The Christian faith is a belief system that must be both caught *and* taught. The psalmist Asaph, for example, advises parents to teach their children about the promises of God.

Give ear, O my people, to my *teaching*;
    incline your ears to the *words of my mouth*!
I will open my *mouth in a parable*;
    I will utter dark *sayings from of old*,
things that we have heard and *known*,
    that our fathers have *told us*.
We will not hide them from their children,
    but *tell to the coming generation*
the glorious deeds of the LORD, and his might,
    and the wonders that he has done.

He established a testimony in Jacob
    and appointed a law in Israel,
which he commanded our fathers

> to *teach to their children*,
>
> that the next generation might know them,
>
> the children yet unborn,
>
> and arise and *tell them to their children*.
>
> PSALM 78:1-6, EMPHASIS ADDED

Furthermore, the apostle Paul told the Christians in Philippi, "Brothers, join in *imitating* me, and keep your eyes on those who walk according to the *example* you have in us" (Philippians 3:17, emphasis added).

In Titus 2:7-8, we see the need to teach *and* model the Christian faith. "Show yourself in all respects to be a *model of good works*, and in *your teaching* show integrity, dignity, and sound speech that cannot be condemned, so that an opponent may be put to shame, having nothing evil to say about us" (emphasis added).

As a parent, you are to model for your children a person who loves Jesus more than anything. This doesn't mean you have to be superhuman; you just need to humble yourself and let the love of Jesus penetrate your heart. It's impossible to love God without first being impacted by God's love. As 1 John 4:19 tells us, "We love, because He first loved us" (NASB).

To love God is to reciprocate the love He has for you. That is what we call a relationship, and that's precisely what you want to model for your kids. You want to show them what your relationship with God looks like.

One way to demonstrate to your children your love for God is through the example of your prayer life.

Let me ask you: What do your prayers look like? Are they frequent or few and far between? Are your prayers eager and persistent, or are they lacking in faith and fervor?

Prayer is one of the most powerful tools we have as Christians. It is our lifeline to God. In his classic book on prayer, Paul Miller writes, "Prayer is simply the medium through which we experience and connect to God."[1] Prayer is a special time of listening to God, praising Him for who He is, confessing our sins, and interceding on behalf of others. Therefore, to love God is to desire to connect with Him in prayer.

King David summed it up beautifully when he penned these words: "As a deer pants for flowing streams, so pants my soul for you, O God. My soul thirsts for God, for the living God. When shall I come and appear before God?" (Psalm 42:1-2).

If you sometimes find it difficult to pray, I recommend you adapt the "Model Prayer" from Matthew 6:9-13, using it as a guide for how and what to pray:

- Bring *adoration* to God (Matthew 6:9).
- Yield *submission* to God (Matthew 6:10).
- Make *petitions* to God (Matthew 6:11).
- Offer *confession* to God (Matthew 6:12).
- Pursue *devotion* to God (Matthew 6:13).

A prayer journal is another helpful tool. I use one myself. It helps me maintain consistency and persistency in my prayers, and it is a great way to share specific prayers with my kids. I challenge you to do your best to model a devoted prayer life to your kids and welcome them to join you in spending time in the presence of God.

This leads to another way to show your children your love for God. The apostle John writes, "Do not love the world or the things in the world. If anyone loves the world, the love of the Father is not in him" (1 John 2:15). Don't overlook this: How you live for (and love) God says everything about you. Some parents might tell their children that they believe in and worship the true and living God, yet their actions reveal that they are more devoted to power, money, or success. This sends mixed messages to children. So examine your heart before God and confess any idols in your life. Teach your family to worship God and Him alone.

Every time you resist temptation or avoid getting sucked into the desires of the world, you are modeling for your kids a love for God. On the other hand, if you love the things of this world, you likely don't love God as much as you think. Jesus affirmed in the Sermon on the Mount that "no one can serve two masters, for either he will hate the one and love the other, or he will be devoted to the one and despise the other. You cannot serve God and money" (Matthew 6:24).

As a Christian parent, you need to lead by example. Think about it this way: I'm a New England Patriots fan—which, by tradition, means that I typically root against the Pittsburgh Steelers. What would my kids think if they saw their dad cheering on the Pats while wearing a Steelers jersey? That wouldn't make sense. And I'll tell you right now, they wouldn't put up with it. They'd probably kick me out of the house!

Maybe they wouldn't, but I think you get my point.

I understand that modeling how a Christian ought to act is much more significant than professing loyalty to a particular team. In other words, don't just *talk* to your kids about your relationship with Christ; *show* them what it means to be a follower of Jesus Christ. Here are a few passages that address what it means to have a personal relationship with Jesus: Matthew 16:24; John 3:16-17, 36; 14:23; Romans 10:9-10; 2 Corinthians 5:17-20; Ephesians 5:1-2; Philippians 3:7-10.

The Second Step: Model a Life Devoted to Growing in Faith and Knowledge

Like many young people throughout history, Gen Z carefully watches their parents' every move. There's not much a parent can get away with these days, especially in a house full of kids. That's certainly the case in my house.

So there is a lot to be said for modeling spiritual disciplines in ways that your children can see, respond to, and put into practice in their own lives. In their book *So the Next Generation Will Know*, Sean McDowell and Jim Wallace stress the importance of this very thing when they say, "We must help young Christians come to know that they know truth—through both correct information and formative practices—so they can live out their beliefs with clarity, consistency, and conviction."[2]

A spiritual practice that every Christian parent should model and teach their kids is reading and growing in knowledge of the Bible. As Paul wrote to his protégé, Timothy, "All Scripture is breathed out by God and profitable for teaching, for reproof, for correction, and for training in righteousness, that the man of God may be complete, equipped for every good work" (2 Timothy 3:16-17).

— — —

I'm friends with two brothers who head up a national ministry designed to empower Christian entrepreneurs in the workplace. The men recalled how, when they were growing up, their dad sat in his chair every morning, read the Bible, and prayed. They said the devotion demonstrated by their father set the tone for them to do the same.

I can still remember when I, as a child, walked into my mother's room to see her propped up in bed reading the Bible. Watching my mom read and study the Scriptures left a lasting impression on me.

But a daily diet of Bible reading is not enough. You also need to demonstrate to your kids that you obey what the Bible says. Look at what 1 John 5:3 explicitly states: "This is the love of God, that we keep His commandments" (NASB). Now, I'm not suggesting that you and I will do precisely what the Bible commands every single time, but we should try our best with the help of the Holy Spirit (Romans 8:13). Because that's what Gen Z needs to see from parents—that the Bible isn't just a resource for *information* but a source of *transformation*.

Keep in mind that God's Word has tremendous power to transform your life when you faithfully read and obey it.

The Bible is

- inspired by God (2 Timothy 3:16-17),
- infallible (Psalm 19:7),
- inerrant (Proverbs 30:5-6), and
- authoritative (Psalm 119:89).

The Bible blesses us with

- sanctification in truth (John 17:17),
- blessing (Luke 11:28),
- victory (Ephesians 6:17),
- spiritual maturity (1 Peter 2:2),
- power (Romans 1:16), and
- guidance (Psalm 119:105).

The Bible gives us a faith that is

- growing (John 6:68-69),
- obedient (1 John 2:5),
- strong (Jude 1:3), and
- prepared (2 Timothy 4:2).

I have always told my children, "The only thing in this world that is infallible—and therefore will not lie to you—is the Word of God."

So maintain a steady diet of the Bible in your daily life. It not only provides invaluable wisdom but also helps mend the brokenhearted and restores the soul.

The Third Step: Model the Value of Attending Church

When churches reopened after the COVID-19 lockdowns, millions of families never returned. Sure, some still felt safer watching services online, but the bulk of those families had simply gotten used to staying at home. When the time came to resume in-person services, the local church was no longer a priority.

Amid all the negative news about Gen Z and faith, one encouraging sign is that Christian Gen Zers exhibit remarkable dedication to church. *Christianity Today* reported that "nearly 6 in 10 evangelical members of Gen Z attend church at least once a week. That's as high as evangelicals older than 75 and statistically higher than baby boomers and those in Generation X. The same pattern emerges among mainline Protestants and Catholics, as well."[3]

That's great news.

Yes, I realize that these numbers refer to only that 30 percent of the Gen Z population that identify as believers. I get that. It's a relatively small number compared with the millions of Gen Zers who *don't* attend church. But you know what? I am confident that the number can grow. Can you imagine what might happen if more parents (like the ones reading this book) made a concentrated effort to invite Gen Zers and their families to church?

My wife and I have seen firsthand the impact that the church has on kids. I can say with all sincerity that we are far better parents today because of the love and support we received from our home church. It's a shame when parents make church nothing more than just another weekend activity (if that).

Gen Z needs to view the church (in many respects) as a second home—a place where they feel safe *and* able to be vulnerable. A place where they can ask tough questions and not feel judged for it. A place where they (and their parents) can learn and develop their spiritual gifts.

So I ask you, Mom and Dad, are you modeling the importance of church in your home?

The Fourth Step: Model the Importance of Community

One summer night I was headed to the dining hall after teaching a session at Summit Ministries. Before I could even grab my tray, a group of students came up and invited me to have dinner with them. After getting my food, I walked over to the young and vibrant group of students who were gesturing to me where to sit.

"Tell me," I asked them, "what's been your favorite experience these past twelve days?"

Without hesitation, every student said it was the community they were cultivating while being at Summit.

That interaction confirmed to me that it doesn't matter what generation you represent. As relational beings, every one of us can benefit from meaningful and lasting relationships.

Gen Zers are looking for transparency and vulnerability in the people they connect with, yet they often struggle with opening themselves up to others. We can blame screens to a certain degree for Gen Z's inability to socialize and make friends. But a big reason why Gen Z lacks community is that their parents do as well.

Gen Z needs to see that you, the parents, have a community of like-minded friends who will pray for you—people you can count on when life gets hard. But the sad truth is that many Gen Z parents don't have that close group of friends. They might have people they hang with from time to time, but they lack a community of fellow Christians who can "build [them] up," as Paul describes in 1 Thessalonians 5:11.

Not long ago, while I was traveling and speaking, a friend in my men's group sent out a group text to report that a massive tree had fallen onto his property. Thankfully, no one was injured, but he didn't have the tools or the manpower to remove the tree from his yard. He needed help.

So how did our brotherhood of believers respond? Did they ignore his request for help? No way! Several of the men leaped into action to help a brother out. *That's* real community. And I know it meant a lot to this man's kids to see their dad's friends come to the family's aid.

That's what your kids want to see. It's what they *need* to see. They need to know that you can rely on a group of trusted friends who have your back, who are there to help you grow in your relationship with God. The writer of Hebrews imparts this wisdom: "And let us consider how to stir up one another to love and good works, not neglecting to meet together, as is the habit of some, but encouraging one another, and all the more as you see the Day drawing near" (Hebrews 10:24-25).

Without a trusted community, young people are more likely to stray from the faith and get caught up in all sorts of things they will later regret. To give your children a positive model, be sure to invest in friendships that matter while helping your kids learn to do the same.

The Fifth Step: Model a Servant's Heart

I can't speak for others, but I love the way I'm treated at Chick-fil-A. Fans of the restaurant—like me—will eagerly tell you that no other fast-food chain can beat Chick-fil-A's "my pleasure" customer service.

But when it comes to the example you set for your kids, how much of that positive attitude do your kids receive from you?

We typically hope and expect service workers to lead with kindness, but serving others is not just about what *other* people have done for *you* lately. It's about what *you* can do to serve *them* right now. In the Sermon on the Mount, Jesus said, "So whatever you wish that others would do to you, do also to them, for this is the Law and the Prophets" (Matthew 7:12). Luke's account offers even more insight into what we know as the Golden Rule:

> If you love those who love you, what benefit is that to you? For even sinners love those who love them. And if you do good to those who do good to you, what benefit is that to you? For even sinners do the same. And if you lend to those from whom you expect to receive, what credit is that to you? Even sinners lend to sinners, to get back the same amount. But love your enemies, and do good, and lend, expecting nothing in return, and your reward will be great, and you will be sons of the Most High, for he is kind to the ungrateful and the evil. Be merciful, even as your Father is merciful.
>
> LUKE 6:32-36

Raising your kids to abide by the Golden Rule is a challenge. After all, even Jesus' disciples found it hard to serve one another. In Mark 9:33-37, as the disciples were journeying to Capernaum, we discover them arguing among themselves about which of them was the greatest. Matthew's account says that after arriving there, the disciples together came to Jesus and asked, "Who is the greatest in the kingdom of heaven?" (Matthew 18:1).

What nerve asking Jesus that! As though He played favorites! Why did the disciples make a big deal about whom Jesus favored the most? They asked this because prominence, in Jewish culture, was a very big deal. A Jew's ranking and position of authority was everything, which helps explain why the disciples argued and tried to get Jesus to establish a pecking order among them.

Let's just say that Jesus wasn't playing along. Instead, "he sat down and called the twelve. And he said to them, 'If anyone would be first, he must be last of all and servant of all.' And he took a child and put him in the midst of them, and taking him in his arms, he said to them, 'Whoever receives one such child in my name receives me, and whoever receives me, receives not me but him who sent me'" (Mark 9:35-37).

Ouch! Can you imagine how small the disciples felt after hearing that from Jesus? Whatever self-confidence they had at that moment likely went right out the window. Jesus confronted His disciples' arrogance by correcting their delusions of greatness. Until that moment, the disciples evaluated greatness in accordance with their authority and standing. According to Jesus, however, the greatness of a person is in proportion to his or her humility, as well as their service to God and others.

Cultivating a heart of service requires that we set aside our own ambitions and empathize with those who need our help (Philippians 2:3-4). There's no doubt that Jesus is our primary example of empathy. He humbled himself by coming into the world as a human—to feel what we feel. And despite entering a world with a history filled with some of the worst behavior imaginable, Jesus still offered up His life so that we could be set free from sin and death.

You can certainly require or demand that your kids serve God and others, but that won't motivate them to do so on their own. Serving out of the abundance of the heart is far more meaningful than operating out of convenience or compulsion. Teach and show Gen Z how to be empathetic by your *example*. Don't just talk the talk; *walk* the talk. And when your son or daughter demonstrates acts of service and kindness, be sure to take note and commend them for it.[4]

As the primary spiritual leader for your kids, model the heart of a servant and teach them to put others' needs above their own.

The Sixth Step: Model How to Defend Your Faith

The shame that many young people feel when talking openly and publicly about their faith speaks to today's so-called "cancel culture" mentality. That same culture, which many Gen Zers subscribe to, suggests that faith—especially Christian faith—is a private matter and has no place in the modern marketplace of ideas. One example of this is YouTube. When you upload a video to the platform, YouTube prompts you to "add your video to a category so viewers can find it more easily." Here are the category options at the time of this writing:

- Film & Animation
- Autos & Vehicles
- Music
- Pets & Animals
- Sports
- Travel & Events
- Gaming
- People & Blogs
- Comedy
- Entertainment
- News & Politics
- How-to & Style
- Education
- Science & Technology
- Nonprofits & Activism

Do you notice anything missing? There's absolutely no category that represents "Faith," "Religion," or "Spirituality." How can that be? How can YouTube completely leave out a category that speaks to billions of people across the globe? In the United States alone, nearly 80 percent of Americans consider themselves religious or spiritual. Yet according to YouTube, it's best to leave that sort of content uncategorized.

YouTube and other media conglomerates seem more interested in having Gen Z focus on sports, their pets, and food than on religious matters.

You know what else? It isn't YouTube's fault.

We, the parents—the Christian adults—have done Gen Z a disservice by not speaking up more on matters of great concern and by not engaging with cultural and moral issues. Gen Z needs to see their parents live not just principled lives but lives full of conviction and passion for issues that are near and dear to our hearts.

The apostle Peter exhorted the early church to "in your hearts honor Christ the Lord as holy, always being prepared to make a defense to anyone who asks you for a reason for the hope that is in you; yet do it with gentleness and respect, having a good conscience, so that, when you are slandered, those who revile your good behavior in Christ may be put to shame" (1 Peter 3:15-16).

I've heard some Christians say that they're not smart enough to intellectually defend what they believe. When I hear this, I encourage believers to not let fear, embarrassment, or any other reason prevent them from sharing God's truth with others. It's okay to say, "I don't know that answer, but I will find out." I've had to say that quite a few times in my own life.

Just make sure that when you do give answers regarding your faith, you are providing reliable information about what you believe and why. *That's* what it means to defend your faith. When someone presents questions or offers an objection to Christianity, believers are compelled by God to give a defense for our faith (see 1 Peter 3:15). The apostle Paul did exactly that throughout his ministry (Acts 22:1; 1 Corinthians 9:3; Philippians 1:7; 2 Timothy 4:16).

Here are some questions for you to consider:

- Have you ever shared your faith in front of your kids?
- Have you ever defended your faith in public?
- Have you ever shared Christ with someone of another faith, or have you spoken with a non-Christian about God's existence, the Resurrection, or the reliability of the Bible?
- Moreover, have you ever used such an experience as a way to teach your kids to do the same?

Moms and dads, your Gen Z kids need to see you confront objections to Christianity and learn from how you handle opposition—especially when so many people seem committed to removing Christianity from modern society.

Parenting Practice

1. List the six steps from this chapter in the order that you feel best speaks to how well you've modeled them for your kids. Consider how you've been a good model in each area and what more you can do to boost your witness.

2. Pray together as a family every day. It doesn't have to be a lengthy time, but make it long enough for each family member to get a chance to pray.

3. Look for opportunities to serve as a family at church or with a local ministry.

4. Make a concerted effort to acknowledge your children when they demonstrate kindness or show empathy.

5. Download a Bible app (like YouVersion) and ask each family member to help pick a reading plan that you can go through together. Discuss each day's reading during dinner. (Also check out the Bible Project's YouTube channel for fun and artistic videos.)

6. Invite some families from church or your neighborhood over to your home for a weekly Bible study.

7. Educate yourself in apologetics. Take a class at church or attend a conference with your family. You can also check out my YouTube channel (Jason P. Jimenez). Some recommended resources on the subject include *I Don't Have Enough Faith to Be an Atheist* by Norman Geisler and Frank Turek (book and study guide) and *The Bible's Answers to 100 of Life's Biggest Questions* by Norman Geisler and Jason Jimenez.

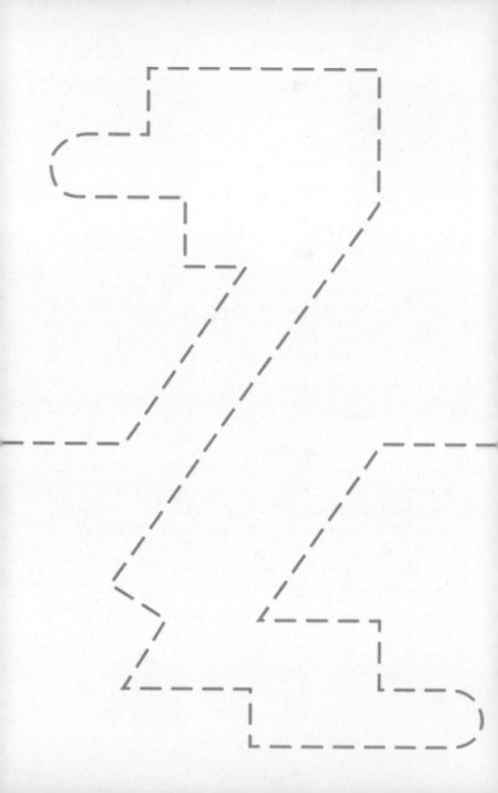

12

FIVE WAYS TO FEED
THEIR FUTURES

SHORTLY AFTER GRADUATING HIGH SCHOOL, I got the urge
to join the military. I was picking up a few items from the grocery
store when I noticed a recruiting office next door. I was only seventeen at the time, so I wasn't sure if I was ready to talk to a recruiter.
But I did anyway.

I was very excited after speaking with the recruiter. He told me
one amazing story after another and gave me some brochures to
take home and show my father. I couldn't wait.

It didn't take long for my dad to shut down my newfound
military aspirations. I remember being really upset and asking him
why he wouldn't sign the papers.

To be fair to my father, and to help you better understand the
situation, I feel like I need to provide some additional context.

Right around the time that I visited the recruitment center, I had just started an internship at my local church. So it wasn't that my dad had something against the military—he was understandably concerned about my *preexisting commitment* to the church.

Ever since I can remember, I've felt drawn to ministry. Yet it never made much sense to me until around the time that I started my internship. Meanwhile, my father and mother (before she passed away) somehow realized that pastoral ministry was my calling in life. Like any good father, my dad was just trying to help me make the best decision and not live to regret my choices. My father knew God hadn't called me to join the military, so he encouraged me to stick with my commitment to the church internship and see what happened.

I'm glad that I listened to my father and that he pointed me in the right direction.

I share this story because if it weren't for my dad's firmness and his faith in my calling to ministry, I believe I would have made a big mistake. My dad's firmness wasn't about him being domineering or a control freak. He was simply guiding me along what he believed was God's path for my life.

INTO THE UNKNOWN

The relationships today between many parents and their Gen Z kids are a lot different—and possibly more volatile—than those of previous generations. Parents are locked in a constant struggle to remain relevant as they prepare their Gen Zers for the future.

I understand that we parents can't know or control the futures of our kids. But I do know that God is sovereign over their futures, and He has placed us in our kids' lives to play a significant role. Parents are a critical element in shaping our children into the men and women God has called them to be.

One of the primary goals of any parent is to teach their children to live and thrive on their own—to help them arrive at adulthood with the maturity necessary to take on whatever challenges might come their way.

Consider for a moment the "growing pains" that most young bodies go through as they develop. The exact growth process and the intensity of the discomfort will vary depending on the child, yet it's a normal part of physically maturing into adulthood. Similarly, if we want to see our children achieve their desired goals in life, they will almost certainly experience some mental and emotional growing pains.

Your kids will experience their fair share of twists and turns in life. They will encounter unexpected roadblocks. Take wrong turns. And most of the time they will insist that they know what they're doing—even when they don't. It's all part of growing up and taking on more freedom and responsibility. In *For Parents Only*, authors Shaunti Feldhahn and Lisa Rice remind parents that as our kids get older, they need more freedom. "The vast majority of kids feel compelled to become their own person, with tastes, values, and goals that may be different from those of their parents—and by the time they hit seventeen years old, the number rises to nearly 100 percent."[1]

As your kids transition into adulthood, they need to be free to make mistakes and to learn from them. They need to experience what it takes to push forward until they get it right. And what happens when they do push through? It's a confidence booster. It's also a great reminder that parents must learn to relinquish some control and put faith in their children's decision-making.

You have to trust that what you taught them in their early years will help them make wise decisions when they're on their own.

Truth is, you can't protect your children from the trials and disappointments of this world, whether it's scraping a knee or getting cut from the team. Our kids will face hardship. They will experience hurt, rejection, and pain. These things are all a part of life.

Every good parent wants what's best for their children. But we can lead our kids down the wrong path if our desires and dreams for them are misguided. If you're guilty of pushing your own agenda on your kids, I encourage you to confess that to God and ask Him to help you surrender their futures to Him. Another important part of the parenting process is to consider the following five areas in which you can help nurture your children's dreams for the future.

Gratitude

Growing up in a culture filled with "me-first" attitudes, Gen Zers find it easy to adopt a consumer mentality. Children who are allowed to prioritize their own needs and wants will become self-centered adults. They will grow up caring about who *they* are in life, with little consideration for others. However, children raised to consider how they might meet the needs of *others* will become more fulfilled adults.

A crucial part of your job is to prevent your children from becoming consumers who care only about themselves. Teach your children what it means to be a contributor. A contributor is someone who exhibits gratitude in life—someone who seeks to solve problems and looks to serve others.

Our children have been given unique gifts and talents. But those abilities aren't meant to benefit only them. Your child's particular set of skills should ideally be used to bless others and help make a difference in the world.

Amy Morin, a licensed clinical social worker and psychotherapist, wrote a piece for *Psychology Today* titled "7 Scientifically Proven Benefits of Gratitude." Here are the seven benefits listed by Dr. Morin:

1. Gratitude opens the door to more relationships.
2. Gratitude improves physical health.
3. Gratitude improves psychological health.
4. Gratitude enhances empathy and reduces aggression.
5. Grateful people sleep better.
6. Gratitude improves self-esteem.
7. Gratitude increases mental strength.[2]

As you can see, instilling an attitude of gratitude in your child's life can be very rewarding. It's so important, in fact, that the apostle Paul tells believers that "giv[ing] thanks in all circumstances" is living in accordance with God's will (1 Thessalonians 5:18).

An Old Testament figure who exemplified a life of gratitude is Joseph. Even after he was sold into slavery, was falsely accused of wrongdoing, and abandoned in prison to die, Joseph still kept the faith. He remained grateful to God for the many blessings he had received, even in the midst of his trials. And guess what? God rewarded Joseph's grateful heart by raising him to a role of prominence wherein he was used to help save two nations!

Something my wife and I do to help instill a sense of gratitude in our children is share with them stories of hardship, such as those published by the nonprofit organization Voice of the Martyrs. In our experience, exposure to real-life testimonies about those who have it far worse helps teach our children to have grateful hearts. Another way to learn gratitude is to discuss (and live out) ways to extend acts of kindness to those around you—in your neighborhood, in school, and at church.

Passions and Interests

Needless to say, no two children are alike. Each has their own passions, and each approaches life in their own unique way.

At this moment in my children's lives, their future interests include becoming a project manager or maybe a counselor, studying to be a professor of literature, owning a bed-and-breakfast (complete with a bakery), and becoming an actor.

Kids' passions can easily change, that's for sure. That's why my wife and I pay much closer attention to *why* they want to do certain things down the road. What kinds of passions do they reveal when talking about a specific subject or career path? Those details are important because what your child is passionate about today can help shed light on future dreams, even at an early age. However, passions and interests can reveal only so much. They are not the ruling factors in determining your child's pathway to success.

As you feed your child's creativity, be sure to spend equal time feeding their curiosity. When my daughter Amy showed an interest in art, we bought her paints and brushes and signed her up for art class. We didn't do it because we somehow knew that Amy would become a professional artist. We did it because of her curiosity.

As Amy has blossomed, so, too, have her passions and curiosities. She's the one who wants to someday teach literature at a university. She still loves to paint, but she now spends most of her time reading and writing. Some might think that her desire to paint has little to do with literature, but the two interests are not mutually exclusive. Both disciplines involve an artistic mindset, creativity, and the ability to conceive and tell a story. When Amy was younger, neither she nor her mom and I envisioned writing in her future. All we knew was that she had a creative and curious mind. In Amy's case, the two go hand in hand.

Thus, a major aspect of nurturing your children's passions is to simply let them try stuff to see what interests them. But this can also get a bit tricky because, all too often, kids are passionate and curious about a *lot* of different things. And as their interests develop, so, too, will their curiosity. They might love to dance.

Or play sports. Perhaps they love English. Or math. Or science. And when they have too many choices to choose from, they can become overwhelmed.

Here's one way to feed your child's curiosity by helping them figure out which passions to pursue: Teach them to problem-find. No, not problem-*solve*. Problem-*find*. Many parents already do a good job of teaching their kids to solve problems for themselves. And there's certainly nothing wrong with that; problem-solving is an important skill. But problem-finding, according to the book *Designing Your Life: How to Build a Well-Lived, Joyful Life*, is also important. In the book, authors Bill Burnett and Dave Evans ask this question: How can people expect to solve their problems if they don't know what problems need solving?

Burnett and Evans then proceed to make their case: "Deciding which problems to work on may be one of the most important decisions you make, because people can lose years (or a lifetime) working on the wrong problem."[3]

This is sadly true of a lot of people. Perhaps it's true of you. To hopefully avoid having your child still solving the wrong problems well into their twenties and thirties, help them problem-find starting *now*. Help your children discover the problems they need to work on now so they can better decide what they want to do later.

Don't worry if your kids are currently in high school and still not sure what they want to do with their lives. Most adults didn't have a clue about their long-term futures when they were teens. Did *you* know what you wanted to do for the rest of your life before you graduated high school? How about your friends?

No, your job is to keep praying for your children and encouraging them along the way as they figure out their future paths. And never forget the promise from God in Psalm 32:8: "I will instruct you and teach you in the way which you should go; I will advise you with My eye upon you" (NASB).

Expectations

The title of Charles Dickens's classic 1861 novel *Great Expectations* is inspired by the character Pip—a poor orphan boy with big dreams of one day becoming a wealthy gentleman. Through many twists and turns, Pip faces a slew of challenges and obstacles. There are times when it seems that all hope is lost for the young lad. Yet, with great resolve, Pip never quits. He keeps pushing forward no matter the setback. He's determined to fulfill the expectations he has set for himself.

The story of Pip is a masterpiece, and not just because Dickens really knew how to tell a story (though he definitely did). I think *Great Expectations* is a classic at least in part because the story speaks to the hearts of young adults. It spoke to the London teenagers who read it in 1861, and it still speaks to the sixteen-year-old reading it on her Kindle today.

Readers identify with Pip's ambitious desire to "be someone" because that same desire exists in all our hearts at some point.

A real-life example of someone who had great expectations is Matt Mullenweg. You might not recognize his name, but you've likely seen his influence. Mullenweg is the guy who helped develop WordPress—the Internet's leading digital content management system, the software that powers more than 40 percent of the world's most popular websites. And he did it when he was only nineteen years old.

Mullenweg is a multimillionaire, and WordPress is worth an estimated few billion dollars. Yet he didn't become a success on his own. Mullenweg attributes much of his success to his dad.

In a post devoted to the life and legacy of Chuck Mullenweg, the so-called "Blog Prince" paid tribute to his father:

> It is impossible to overstate the influence my father has had on every part of my life: Why did I play saxophone?

Dad did. Computers and programming? Dad did. Travel? He was frequently stationed overseas and even when we didn't visit he would always bring back a cool gift for myself and my sister. He drove me to the HAL-PC office (local non-profit) every weekend where I'd learn so much fixing people's broken computers and being exposed to open source for the first time. . . . We were in a father/son bowling league. I remember admiring his work ethic so much: he'd get up before dawn every morning and put on a suit, grab his briefcase, and go to work.[4]

Undoubtedly, Matt Mullenweg's father played an integral role in feeding his passions and interests. At the same time, there is no way the son would or could have developed WordPress if he hadn't set forth certain expectations for himself. But he did—and because he did, he was able to attain those goals.

I'm not suggesting that your sons or daughters are destined to become multimillionaires. Who knows? But I can promise you this: Your children will never reach their goals if they never set them. Many child psychologists and teachers would agree that kids who take the initiative to set goals are (by far) the most successful and accomplished in life.[5]

You've probably heard the saying, "A journey of a thousand miles begins with a single step." If your child's journey involves turning their skills and talents into their livelihood, then he or she must be willing to take that first step—and then keep going.

Expectations, however, come with their own set of risks. And with risks come potential failures. Yet we also know that it's often in times of failure or disappointment, when our faith is tested, that we turn to and lean on God for comfort, guidance, and strength (see 1 Peter 1:6-7).

It's hard to watch our kids experience pain or disappointment.

Our first reaction is to dive in and rescue them. But that's often not the best course of action. A growing body of research shows that children's neurodevelopment suffers when they are unable to assess risks on their own and therefore develop the tools necessary to act independently.[6]

It's tough, but it's true: Parents *have* to let their kids experience failure. Setbacks and failures are not only an inevitable part of life, but to face (and eventually overcome) them is good for our kids. It teaches them resilience. It builds character. It helps them accept defeat. And it's in those moments of defeat that you, the parents, are there to love them and reassure them that to fail doesn't mean they *are* failures.

So try not to interfere when your son is setting specific goals or expectations for himself. Instead, provide the attention and guidance he needs without creating his plans for him. Likewise, you can advise your daughter without deciding for her what goals she needs to pursue. If she falls short or messes up her timeline, it's not the end of the world. It's not on you to accomplish each goal, but it is on you to cheer for your children and to motivate them to keep going until they reach the finish line.

Patience

As I write this section, my family and I are at the beach for some R&R. Earlier this afternoon, I couldn't help but overhear two boys (both no older than twelve) complaining to their parents. Sitting in their beach chairs, the boys were hungry, hot, and bored, so the parents suggested that the pair go play in the ocean for a few more minutes before the family went to grab lunch. The boys, however, didn't like that idea and continued to complain.

The mother finally reached her breaking point. She shot out of her chair and announced, "Whatever! Just quit your whining. We'll go get something to eat." The father didn't like that one bit, but no one else seemed to care. The kids ran off to lunch, leaving their dad to carry the family's beach gear by himself.

I'm not sure whether it was sunburn or the fact that he was steaming mad that made the father look so red.

I mention this episode at the beach because it speaks to the need for patience. Think about it—how patient do you suppose those kids will be later in life when they're trying to get into the college of their choice? Or when they're interviewing for a job? Will they have the patience to endure some hard times, or will they give up and quit?

Robert Kearns was a guy who didn't quit, no matter how hard and how long he had to fight. Who was Robert Kearns, you ask? He was a physics professor who invented intermittent windshield wipers.

In 1964, Kearns filed the first of numerous patents for his invention. It wasn't long before Kearns approached the Ford Motor Company and other major car companies about implementing his revolutionary windshield wipers. Instead of licensing Kearns's technology, Ford—and eventually other auto manufacturers— imitated his wiper designs and began installing them on their own cars in 1969. Kearns wasn't happy about Ford essentially stealing his invention, so he sued the auto industry giant for patent infringement. Ford's defense team came out strong, insisting that *their* windshield wipers were their own idea.

The legal system eventually decided that Ford was lying, but guess how long it took for Kearns to receive justice? His lawsuit against Ford wasn't resolved until 1990. A subsequent suit against Chrysler wasn't resolved until 1995. That's more than thirty years after Kearns filed his first patent! But Kearns stuck with it. He had both thirty years of patience and the corresponding resolve to demonstrate that he was the original creator of intermittent windshield wipers. After his long and arduous legal battles, the courts finally sided with Kearns and awarded him millions in compensation. (Kearns ended up representing himself in court, and the stress of the legal proceedings reportedly cost him both his marriage and his mental health—keep that in mind if your patience and resolve ever lead you to go up against some of the world's biggest companies in court!)

So the next time you're driving in a light rain, you can thank good ol' Robert Kearns for creating intermittent windshield wipers. And think of the patience he must have had—to not only invent those wipers but also to take on the major car manufacturers by himself.

Kearns's story is an extreme example, but that's what we want to see in our kids, right? We want them to keep pushing. To not give up. To remain patient and carry on no matter the challenge. The problem is that Gen Z exists in a time and culture of instant gratification. As a hyperconnected generation, they've learned to expect quick fixes and can't survive without next-day delivery. (To be honest, neither can their parents at times!)

But life doesn't always work that way. We all need to exhibit patience. Patience is not only a virtue but also an attribute that will produce other fruitful qualities in your child's life—both now and in the future. Paul affirms the value of patience in Romans 5:4: "Endurance [patience] produces character, and character produces hope."

It's hard to expect your children to succeed in life if they're impatient. How will they ever achieve their goals or exceed their expectations if they lack the patience to follow through? A big part of an employee's success is their ability to get along with their colleagues in the workplace. This requires patience—sometimes a ton of it.

Therefore, as you help cultivate your children's gifts and talents, don't neglect teaching them the virtue and the value of patience. Look for opportunities to help your Gen Z children be more patient, especially when things are out of their control or don't pan out the way they had hoped.

Dedication

Your son or daughter might be highly talented, but talent alone is not enough. Your children also need dedication and the willingness to work hard; to hone their craft as much as it takes. They need to devote the necessary time and practice—and make the sacrifices required—to not only get better but also excel. Gaining practical experience and taking ownership of the results are essential in the development of any child (or adult!).

When I was growing up, my Grandpa Jimenez had an idea: He wanted to construct a wall around our one-acre property. My extended family, you see, lived in a duplex. On one side was my immediate family, and in the other half of the house lived my grandparents and aunt.

I can't recall precisely when we began building the wall. I think it was the summer of 1988 or '89, which means I was nine or ten years old at the time. But that didn't matter to my grandfather. To him I was an able body ready to be shaped into a hard worker. My size and relative lack of strength didn't deter Grandpa from waking me every morning to dig trenches, mix cement, and level bricks.

It took us a year or so to complete the wall, but I believe it was worth it. My grandpa taught me what it means to be dedicated to a task and remain steadfast until it's complete. I'm grateful to him for teaching me the value of hard work.

A negative stereotype regarding Gen Z is that they lack resilience and grit. Some have gone so far as to dub them the "Complaining

Generation." Remember the two boys at the beach I told you about earlier? When things get too hard or uncomfortable for Gen Zers like them, they tend to complain and even give up rather than persevere. This is partially the result of parents who would rather pamper their kids than stick to their resolve.

The lesson? Don't be too soft with your kids. Teach them the value of hard work. Renowned inventor Thomas Edison is typically credited with the famous adage "Genius is 1 percent inspiration and 99 percent perspiration."

Don't worry, parents—putting your kids to work isn't child abuse. In fact, instilling in your kids the value of hard work and perseverance can make all the difference in the world. Those who remain dedicated to a task will stand out above the rest. Dedication often makes the difference between those who succeed in life and those who don't.

Please don't underestimate the value of the chores you assign your kids or the hours of practice required to improve in a particular craft or skill. Each step your children take to complete a job or move up in the rankings is one step closer to achieving their goals and living their dreams. Proverbs 12:14 tells us, "From the fruit of his mouth a man is satisfied with good, and the work of a man's hand comes back to him."

As you encourage your children to remain dedicated to pursuing God's calling on their lives, keep in mind a few additional tips:

1. Never underestimate what God can do through you.
2. Never forget the turning points that led you to where you are today.
3. Never rely on the path of least resistance.
4. Never shirk your responsibilities. Instead, be faithful and committed to finishing what you set out to do.

5. Never believe life is all about being successful. Your success in life is about honoring God with what He has given you.

Parenting Practice

1. Evaluate how you handle the emotional and spiritual "growing pains" in your kids' lives. Make the adjustments necessary to avoid being an intrusive parent.

2. Designate a few appropriate tasks for each child in your home and have them complete those tasks with minimal help. Afterward, consider how each child did and share any relevant lessons.

3. Following the task above, create a chore chart for each of your kids and hold them accountable for completing their daily tasks.

4. Spend some time with your older kids (generally those ten and up) discussing what they are passionate about. For teenagers, have them take an assessment by searching for "spiritual gifts test" at FocusOnTheFamily.com.

5. Use the five areas listed in this chapter—gratitude, passions and interests, expectations, patience, and dedication—to help prepare your children for their respective futures.

6. Allow your kids to help plan your next family outing or vacation.

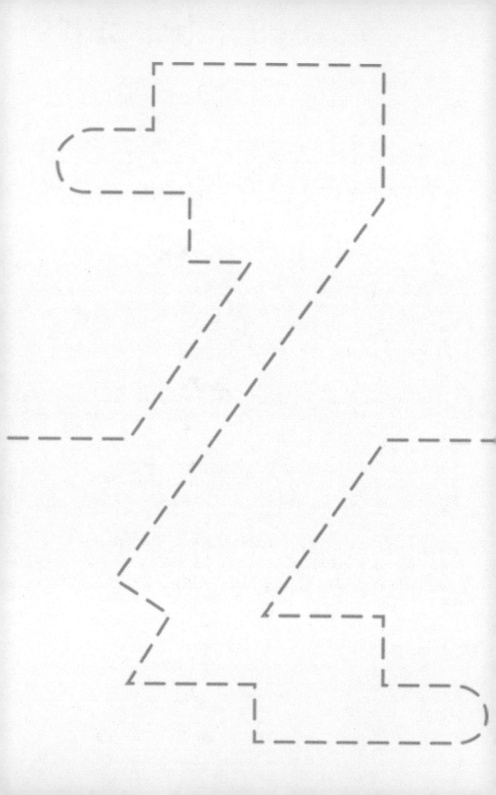

13

SANITY FOR SINGLE PARENTS

IF YOU'RE READING THIS CHAPTER, it likely means you're a single parent. However you've found yourself in this situation, I'm very grateful that you are there for your kids. I can't begin to imagine how hard it is to raise a family by yourself. I promise you, dear reader, that God sees your struggles. You are not alone. I care so much about single parents that I wanted to add this chapter just for you.

For years, my wife and I have had the fortune to come alongside hundreds of single parents to love them, serve them, and offer biblical support and counsel. I don't need to tell you how demanding your job is as a single parent. Raising children on your own is one of the hardest things to go through. Not only are you often managing a roller coaster of your own emotions, but you're also trying to remain strong for your kids so that they, too, can continue to be strong.

This makes me think of Sean.

Sean was part of a group I was leading. I remember when Sean, whose divorce took place when his kids were little, unburdened himself by telling the other group members how he was trying to keep it all together on the outside—yet on the inside, he was coming undone.

"One day, I wake up with a solid outlook on life," he said. "The next day I wake up with absolutely no desire to parent my kids or do anything that requires me to take responsibility for anything."

I'd heard this before. Sean might have felt all alone, but he was simply describing the highs and lows common to single parenting.

I'm no doctor, but I understand what ails you. Wherever you find yourself, I want to prescribe five daily doses of sanity to help keep you moving forward.

FIVE DAILY DOSES OF SANITY

The First Dose: God Is Not Blind

God sees your struggles.

He knows your fears (even the ones tucked away in the back of your mind). He's not clueless about the worries that rob you of sleep. God knows how hard you work to pay your bills and put food on the table. He sees and loves every one of the approximately 10 million households in America that are single-parent families. He's well aware that more than 20 million children in America are raised by single parents.

And let me say this in particular to the single mothers: God knows that 80 percent of those kids are raised by moms like you. He knows about the millions of children who grow up without a loving dad. He sees the hardships your kids experience and the longings they feel.

I think of Stephanie, a single mom in her mid-thirties, who summed it up pretty well: "As a single mom, I go to bed every night totally exhausted after a long day of taking care of my three kids. I do so much, yet I still feel like I'm not doing enough for my kids."

I think of Liam, an eighth grader, who told me that he often hears his mother crying in her bedroom at night.

I think of a forty-five-year-old mom, divorced and raising five kids, who shared with a group of pastors the turmoil she goes through every time her kids return home after spending the weekend with their father. She recounted that the whole time her kids are away, she prays that they won't be yelled at. And when they do return home, this working mom has a series of exercises from her counselor to help "detox" her kids after they've spent time with their toxic dad.

Yet by the time her kids are feeling better, she has to turn around and send them back to their father, essentially undoing all her work from the previous two weeks.

"Words cannot express how emotionally draining it is to go through that with my kids every other week," she told us, fighting to hold back her tears.

No matter what you are going through, rest assured that God knows all about it and wants you to trust Him with your needs. As the apostle Peter tells us, "[Cast] all your anxieties on him, because he cares for you" (1 Peter 5:7).

Take heart in knowing that your problems are not too much for Jesus to handle. He wants you to come to Him. Jesus lovingly instructed His followers: "Come to me, all who labor and are heavy laden, and I will give you rest" (Matthew 11:28).

I'd like you to hear this sound advice presented in Dallas Willard's book *Life without Lack*:

> Having risen in praise and thankfulness, then you pray
> for yourself, for the people in your life, and for the things
> you are facing that day. Declare your dependence upon

God, asking him to remove all fear and to fill you with his love for your life and all that enters it. This is where you move from praise to genuine love for the life God has given you. Do you love your life? Does the love of God come through you to everything you deal with in your life? This is how you will carry Christ through the day. So if you have specific concerns, call them out, lay them before the Lord, and submit them to his care.[1]

The Second Dose: Keep It Cool

In single-parent homes, there are often two extremes at play: The parent is either fighting for complete *compliance* or bending over backward to avoid *defiance*.

Single parents can get caught up in extremes because they are so busy doing double duty at home. Be that as it may, neither of the two extremes works well with raising kids.

Kids don't thrive in a home run like a prison, and they certainly don't flourish if they are the ones calling the shots. That's why keeping it cool no matter how stressed things get in your home life is extremely important. How you respond to problematic situations or attitudes will help set the tone in your home, and setting a good example will prepare your kids to do the same.

But things will not always work out this way. The reality is that you will sometimes lose your cool. You will not always set the best example. Such is life.

Yes, you will make mistakes, but how you respond to those mistakes and how you look to the God of grace will leave a lasting impression on your kids.

At the end of the day, you are teaching your kids *resilience*.

Resilience is defined, at least in part, as "the ability of a person to adjust to or recover readily from illness, adversity, major life changes, etc."[2] By remaining composed and maintaining a positive outlook on life, you're not demanding compliance from your kids or losing control because of their defiance—instead you're teaching your kids how to be resilient.

In her book *Resilient Kids: Raising Them to Embrace Life with Confidence*, author and educator Kathy Koch says it's important for parents to help their kids learn from challenging experiences. Koch explains that there are several different types of resilience, including *physical, social, emotional, intellectual,* and *spiritual* resilience. And if your children are going to experience the benefits of all types of resilience in all areas of their lives, they first need to see them lived out in *your* life.[3]

That won't happen, however, if you are frequently floundering, losing your cool, or busy making excuses for yourself or your kids. Those sorts of behaviors won't set you up as a positive role model. Instead, you need to sit back, gather your thoughts, and gain a clear, biblical perspective of how God wants you to respond to your kids. Is it with more panic and anxiety, or more patience and understanding?

In short, the more you rest in God, the more relaxed you will be in life, which is far better for everyone.

The Third Dose: See the Beauty

Imagine what would happen if, instead of only seeing mounting problems, your eyes were opened to the beautiful presence of God in the mundane activities of everyday life.

It's easy to be so fixated on your family's immediate messes that you miss the little treasures and wonderful moments that exist amid life's pandemonium. A healthy daily exercise, and one I know you will love, involves looking for everyday beauty. As a friend of mine likes to say, "Seek out the charmful moments of everyday life. You can't miss them."

What's so great about finding beauty in everyday life is that it leads to a thankful heart. It reminds you that there is more to life than picking up the pieces after a painful loss or a broken relationship.

The effects of divorce, for example, can emotionally strain your children and exact a physical toll. So as your kids deal with a broad range of conflicting emotions, help them see the beauty that exists all around them—even in the darkest and most depressing of times.

For instance, we all need to experience the beauty of God's comfort in times of loneliness, or the beauty of forgiveness when someone close no longer holds our faults against us.

I know from experience that the beauty of hope can still be found amid the darkness of sorrow. When I was fifteen, my mother was killed in a car accident. I can still remember the horrible feelings of pain and despair. For years I wrestled with the question *What good can come from all this?*

Looking back, I can honestly say that the Lord was so good and so faithful to me. That doesn't mean that it was easy for my family—especially my father. He went from having a loving wife and partner in raising their four boys to being a single dad overnight.

But you know what? Even after that tragic loss, my family still tasted the beauty of God.

Hear this beautiful promise: "And after you have suffered a little while, the God of all grace, who has called you to his eternal glory in Christ, will himself restore, confirm, strengthen, and establish you" (1 Peter 5:10).

The Fourth Dose: Remain Open

Let me ask you something: How many of life's burdens are you carrying all on your own?

Here's the thing—you are not meant to carry your burdens alone. It's impossible. After all, the apostle Paul instructs followers of Jesus to "bear one another's burdens, and thereby fulfill the law of Christ" (Galatians 6:2, NASB).

In Greek, the word translated "burden" here is *baros*, which can also be translated "weight." Paul is saying that we shouldn't have to carry our most crushing challenges alone. So let the people who love you help lift you up. Seek help from those who can carry some of your burdens. And don't be embarrassed to ask.

At the same time, be open with your children. The last thing you want to do is shut them out of your life. Regular, meaningful conversations with your kids will help unlock their hearts and bond your family together.

Think of it this way: When you are real with your kids, there's a greater likelihood that they will behave the same way with you. But if you are standoffish, it will likely lead to distance from your kids and weaken your family bond.

When a nuclear family splinters, no matter the reasons, it creates instability. And if one or both of the parents eventually remarries, it introduces a new set of challenges. Every child needs and wants to experience feelings of love and a sense of security at home, and this is especially true for children from broken homes.

They've likely dealt with plenty of instability and doubt already. What they need now, from you, is a parent they can count on—someone they can believe in. I have found that single parents who remain open about the problems in their families have a far better chance of repairing once-broken relationships.

Consider including in your daily prayers a request that God will help you create an atmosphere of openness and acceptance in your home.

The Fifth Dose: Spend (Your Time) Wisely

No one likes to be in debt, but if you are not wise with your spending, there's a good chance you will be.

The same is true about your time. It can be hard to set aside time as a family, and this can lead to increased frustration, especially if you're a single parent.

For example, a single mom named Megan shared with me how she agonized over every decision she had to make. "It can get pretty overwhelming at times," she said. "I'm trying my best, but I feel like I never have enough time with my kids."

A way to get your mind in the game each day is to begin the morning with prayer. That might sound pretty basic, but prayer is your most valuable tool as a Christian. God wants us to go directly to Him with all our problems.

Begin by asking the Lord to help calm your spirit and give you the wisdom needed to make wise decisions for your family. It can be as simple and straightforward as this prayer:

> *Heavenly Father, thank You for loving me. I come before Your holy presence to ask that You give me the wisdom I need as a single parent to do what is right for my kids. Help settle my heart so that I may not lose sight of what You are doing in my family. Give me the faith necessary to follow Your instructions. In Jesus' name, amen.*

Another way to help ease your stress is to set aside time for *thinking*. Again, this might seem obvious, but it's common for parents under pressure—such as single parents—to plunge ahead without giving their actions much thought.

Instead of being in constant motion all day, take some time to think *first* about what needs to be done and why. If you need to carve out some time on the calendar to gather your thoughts, then do it. Just as important—if not more so—if you need to move back a meeting or cancel an appointment in order to spend time with your kids, then do it.

Make time on your calendar for your family.

Finally, reach out to a few trusted advisers in your life and use them as a sounding board. Ask them to hold you accountable—to ensure that you are wise in guarding your time as a family. The Bible says, "Where there is no guidance, a people falls, but in an abundance of counselors there is safety" (Proverbs 11:14).

As I hope you've realized, being a single parent doesn't mean you are on your own. The Lord is *always* with you, and He has given you everything you need to love and lead your kids.

Know this: You *will* fail sometimes. We all do. But don't quit. Don't give up. Keep taking these daily doses of sanity and look to a better future for you and your kids.

May the Lord of peace give you His peace—at all times and in every way.

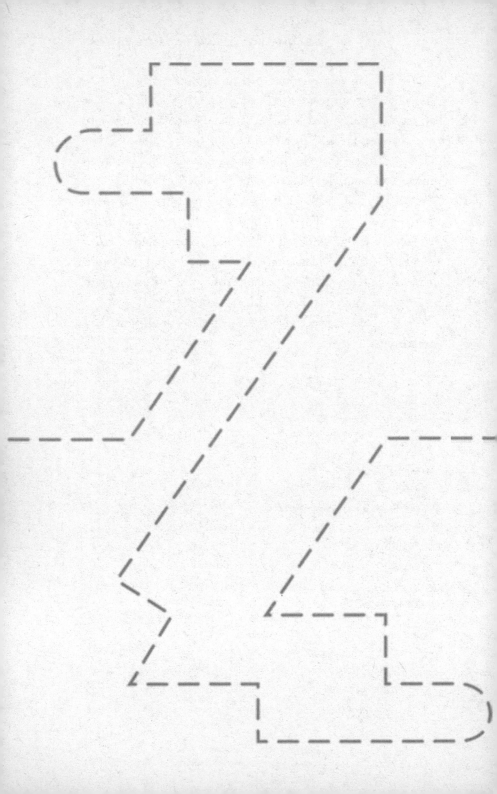

Conclusion

Feeling Stuck in a Never-Ending Maze?

NO ONE LIKES to get stuck.

It doesn't matter whether it's being stuck on a math problem or stuck in traffic—which, by the way, is the worst! And what about getting stuck in a real-life maze with no idea what to do? I can't imagine!

"We've been stuck here for four hours and have no idea how to get out."

That was the 911 call from a family stuck somewhere in a giant corn maze. It started as an exciting adventure, but now they were pleading for help. The ordeal was a terrifying experience for the whole family.

Do you sometimes feel like that family stuck in a corn maze?

You've just finished reading *Parenting Gen Z*, and instead of feeling refreshed and ready to implement what you've learned, maybe you feel—well, let's just be real—like a loser.

Sure, you've gained some insights about Gen Z and some tips on exercising your parental authority, but you still feel stuck because you're not sure if you can implement what you've learned. You might even still be carrying some guilt from past mistakes.

Maybe you lack the confidence to believe you can really improve your parenting.

If that's how you feel, I get it. You're definitely not alone. But consider this: You've made it this far. This tells me that despite feeling stuck, you're still searching for answers and willing to do what it takes to be the parent your family needs.

It's easy to look at other parents and wonder why you can't be more like them.

But you know what? You are *you*. Not *them*.

Don't waste your time fixating on other people. Fix your eyes on Jesus and remind yourself that God has given you the *right* kids. It wasn't a mistake. There were no oversights.

Your children are a gift, and God has distinctively empowered you to love and care for them as only you can. Hold fast to that truth. Instead of questioning and doubting your parenting, I want you to answer this question truthfully: What will you do with the information and advice in this book? How will it change your attitude and approach to parenting?

I realize that as you're reading this, you might be teetering on the verge of a nervous breakdown. Allow me to offer you some good news: Even though you might lack direction—perhaps you have no idea what your next move is—never doubt that God has a plan for you. You might experience many twists and turns, dead ends, and do-overs in your parenting journey, yet always remember that God will never leave you stranded.

Just like a good maze is designed with a solution, God can make a way out of the mess your family might be in. As Christians, we have the confidence that God, who is in us, is infinitely mightier than Satan, who rules the world (see 1 John 4:4). In the very next chapter, John further boosts our confidence: "Everyone who has been born of God overcomes the world. And this is the victory that has overcome the world—our faith" (1 John 5:4).

As you survey your situation, are you about to give up? Are you going to stop asking God to guide and direct your family down the path you should go?

Of course not! Our faith in Jesus is far greater and more robust than the pressures, trials, and disappointments that the world offers.

Sure, you've made your fair share of mistakes in your parenting. We all have. I've shared with you some of my own blunders as a dad. But here's some good news that you and I need to hold on to as children of God: The Bible says that God's grace is sufficient, and His power is made perfect in times of weakness (see 2 Corinthians 12:9).

What does that mean? It means that Jesus' grace is greater than our sins, and He will give us the strength to overcome any obstacle.

So stay the course. And to help you do that, I want to leave you with three uplifting messages of encouragement.

MESSAGE ONE: YOUR INFLUENCE IS IRREPLACEABLE

I'd like to introduce you to two parents you might have never heard of. Their names are Amram and Jochebed, and they were the parents of Moses—the man who became probably the greatest prophet in Israel's history.

At the time of Moses' birth, Amram and Jochebed were living under oppression and slavery in Egypt. Given that Pharaoh had decreed the death of all male Hebrew babies, they were forced to make a decision no parent ever wishes to make: They gave up their son, hoping his life would be spared in the end.

We are told several things about Moses' parents in Hebrews 11:23: "By faith Moses, when he was born, was hidden for three months by his parents, because they saw that the child was beautiful, and they were not afraid of the king's edict."

First, they had faith in God. Amram and Jochebed held on to their faith and trusted God to protect their family. They refused to give in to Pharaoh's decree. Second, they loved their son and knew that God had a special plan for his life. Third, Moses' parents were proactive. They hid their son for three months, and the book of Exodus tells us that Jochebed constructed a floating basket for her precious son, placed it in the Nile River, and trusted that God would guide him to safety.

Although Moses' parents didn't raise their son to adulthood, the love and faith they demonstrated during his first few months of life led to his future as the one who led Israel out of bondage in Egypt.

That's the power of a parent's influence.

My friend Caleb Kaltenbach shares some great insights on the power of influence in his book *Messy Truth*. "Having influence in another person's life is tremendously valuable," he writes. "The more influence you have with someone, the more weight your words and actions carry."[1]

Your children might have many people they look up to—but as their father or mother, you play the most vital and pivotal role. How awesome is that? So rather than waste time sulking about the problems that hinder your relationships with your kids, look for ways to take what you've learned from this book and use your influence to improve those relationships.

MESSAGE TWO: YOUR KIDS DON'T NEED AN "EXPERT" PARENT

Parenting books can be overwhelming.

As I was writing this book, I probably referred to at least fifty other books on parenting, if not many more. Let me tell you, there were plenty of times when I felt unworthy to address these topics.

There were times when I questioned whether I was as good at parenting as the authors I was reading; at other times, I found myself feeling guilty for not implementing something that other authors said I should be doing consistently with my kids.

Sometimes I had a recurring thought: *How much better off would my kids be if this author or that expert were their dad?*

I share these thoughts with you to say that you should let go of any feelings of inadequacy you have about your parenting. Your parenting philosophy may not be as thorough or comprehensive as you'd like, but I give you permission to cut yourself some slack.

Your love for your kids isn't measured by the number of parenting books you've read. Your kids aren't looking for someone who has all the answers. (As a matter of fact, most Gen Zers find it annoying to live with a know-it-all.) No, your kids look to you, their parent, because you are the one who knows their hearts as well as or better than anyone else.

Parents have a natural ability to understand how God has gifted their children, to recognize their unique purposes and personalities, and to know just what their children need in order to feel loved and cared for. As Proverbs 20:5 says, "The purpose in a man's heart is like deep water, but a man of understanding will draw it out."

This passage praises the cleverness, skill, and insight required to extract from a person their genuine emotion. This kind of understanding is at the heart of parenting. Understanding a child's heart is like exploring a cavern deep beneath the surface, and God has given you skills that enable you to uncover the intentions and motives of your child.

Take a moment to reflect on what you've learned from this book and what you will do about it. I hope you are encouraged by the fact that you are better prepared as a parent than when you first started reading.

MESSAGE THREE: LET OTHERS SPEAK INTO YOUR CHILDREN'S LIVES

One day I was talking with one of my boys after he had spent time with a few people from church. During our conversation, it became clear that the people close to my son knew more about his current situation than I did.

He told me their advice and how much it meant to him. I don't want to admit it, but rather than being thankful that my son had people he could turn to besides his mother and me, I was jealous and resentful about the whole thing.

Why didn't my son come to me? Does he not respect me? Does he not think I love him? Does he not trust what I have to say?

Yet as we continued to talk, I remember asking the Holy Spirit to work in my heart. The last thing I wanted was to let my jealousy spoil the mood.

And that's when a wave of guilt swept over me.

I need to be grateful for the people God has placed in my son's life. He may not always come to me with his problems, but as long as he knows I love him and he's seeking godly counsel, that's good enough for me.

The bottom line is that our children need godly voices from outside the family who can speak into their lives.

STAYING THE COURSE

Dear reader, though you might feel trapped in a maze or under a cloud of disappointment that hovers over your family, please remember that it's often in times of hardship that God is actively molding and shaping you.

Sometimes we miss what God is doing *inwardly* (spiritually) with our kids because we are too concerned with their *outward* progress. It reminds me of a quote by the great Bible teacher

Oswald Chambers: "God's aim looks like missing the mark because we are too short-sighted to see what He is aiming at."[2]

Sometimes it might not seem like your parenting is making a difference. But it is. Paul mentions this amazing truth in his second letter to the Corinthians: "And we all, with unveiled face, beholding the glory of the Lord, are being transformed into the same image from one degree of glory to another. For this comes from the Lord who is the Spirit" (2 Corinthians 3:18).

You *are* being conformed to the image of Christ (Romans 8:29), and the negative emotions you are experiencing do *not* define you. Instead, allow God to use your doubts and insecurities to help you grow stronger in the faith.

Your children are precious gifts given by God for you to support, encourage, and ultimately send forth into the world to serve and glorify Him. Therefore, pray daily for your children's moral and spiritual maturity. Pray that they won't fall prey to Satan's deceptions (Acts 26:18; 1 Corinthians 7:5; 2 Corinthians 2:11; 11:3-4; 2 Thessalonians 2:9-10) but that they would take every opportunity to live in accordance with God's will for their lives (see Ephesians 5:15-17).

— — —

We've covered a lot of ground concerning your role as a parent. I hope you won't just set this book aside and quickly forget what you've learned. I said this in the introduction and will repeat it to you now: God has given you everything you need (2 Peter 1:3-9) to get the job done in raising your children. (Yes, even if you are raising them by yourself.)

The Bible is clear that God will keep you from stumbling (Jude 1:24), and—as you remain faithful to your calling as a Christian parent—you will reap the rewards of your labor (Ephesians 6:8).

Parenting will always have its highs and lows. There will be seasons of reaping followed by seasons of barrenness. Sometimes you'll feel like you have this parenting thing down pat. Other times you'll feel like you're the worst parent ever.

One day your role will shift from caretaker and guardian to mentor and friend, but you'll never retire from being a parent. Your children need you to help them navigate a hostile culture. You can do this, Mom and Dad. I believe in you.

Acknowledgments

I AM GRATEFUL to the entire team at Focus on the Family for their unyielding support, prayers, and professional guidance along the way.

Jim Daly, I am indebted to you for backing my books and ministry. It has meant the world to me.

Larry Weeden, you've been a great mentor to me. Thank you for giving me the privilege to write and minister to parents through Focus on the Family.

Danny Huerta, it's been a privilege working with you, my friend. Your support has been a trusted anchor, and I look forward to being in God's service together as we seek to equip more families.

Jeff and Kelly from the publishing team, you two have been rock stars! I appreciate how you kept me on track and directed me toward the light at the end of the tunnel.

Robin Bermel, I deeply appreciate the vision that you and the team at Tyndale have to empower more families with the gospel of Christ.

To my best friend and the one I get to share my life with, Celia: Without your love, wisdom, and lasting contribution to my life, I wouldn't be the man, husband, dad, writer, speaker—pretty much anything—that I am today. You are the glue to our family, and I cannot begin to express the joy you bring to our four children and me. It's been an honor raising our kids together!

And last, to my kiddos: Tyler, Amy, Jackson, and Hailey. I wouldn't have been able to write this book if it weren't for the love and respect you show for your mom and me. Raising and loving you guys has been the most incredible experience of my life. I am both humbled and honored to be your dad.

Notes

INTRODUCTION: GEN Z PARENTS ARE OVERWHELMED

1. "The Most Up-to-Date Pornography Statistics," Covenant Eyes, January 3, 2022, https://www.covenanteyes.com/pornstats. Accessed October 18, 2022.

CHAPTER ONE: WHO IS GEN Z?

1. Caroline Avery, "Generation Z: The School Shooting Generation," *The Spokesman-Review*, May 26, 2018, https://www.spokesman.com/stories /2018/may/26/generation-z-the-school-shooting-generation. Accessed February 8, 2021.
2. Twenty One Pilots, "Stressed Out," track 2 on *Blurryface*, Warner Music Group, Atlantic Records & Fueled by Ramen, 2015.
3. "Resident Population in the United States in 2021, by Generation," Statista, https://www.statista.com/statistics/797321/us-population-by -generation. Accessed October 21, 2022.
4. "US Population by Age and Generation in 2020," Knoema, April 16, 2020, https://knoema.com/infographics/egyydzc/us-population-by-age -and-generation-in-2020. Accessed April 8, 2021.
5. "900 Voices from Gen Z, America's Most Diverse Generation," *New York Times*, March 22, 2019, https://www.nytimes.com/interactive/2019/us /generation-z.html. Accessed March 5, 2021.
6. Jessica Rapp, "Into Z Future: Understanding Generation Z, the Next Generation of Super Creatives," Innovation Group (JWT Intelligence and Snap Inc., 2019), https://assets.ctfassets.net/inb32lme5009/5DFlqKVGId mAu7X6btfGQt/44fdca09d7b630ee28f5951d54feed71/Into_Z_Future _Understanding_Gen_Z_The_Next_Generation_of_Super_Creatives _.pdf. Accessed January 3, 2021.

7. Daniel LeDuc, "Who Is Generation Z? Meet the Post-Millennial and Most Diverse Generation," *Trust Magazine* (The Pew Charitable Trusts), May 20, 2019, https://www.pewtrusts.org/en/trust/archive/spring-2019/who-is -generation-z. Accessed March 15, 2021.

8. Ryan P. Burge, "Gen Z and Religion in 2021," *Religion in Public* (blog), June 15, 2022, https://religioninpublic.blog/2022/06/15/gen-z-and-religion -in-2021. Accessed October 18, 2022.

9. Octavio Esqueda, "What Every Church Needs to Know about Generation Z," *Talbot* (Biola University blogs), November 14, 2018, https://www.biola .edu/blogs/talbot-magazine/2018/what-every-church-needs-to-know-about -generation-z.

10. Rod Dreher, *The Benedict Option: A Strategy for Christians in a Post-Christian Nation* (New York: Penguin Publishing Group, Kindle Edition, 2017), 12.

11. Kathy Koch, *Screens and Teens: Connecting with Our Kids in a Wireless World* (Chicago: Moody Publishers, 2015).

12. Elizabeth Drescher, *Choosing Our Religion: The Spiritual Lives of America's Nones* (New York: Oxford University Press, 2016), 42–47.

13. Kim Parker, Juliana Menasce Horowitz, and Anna Brown, "Americans' Complex Views on Gender Identity and Transgender Issues" (Pew Research Center, June 28, 2022), https://www.pewresearch.org/social -trends/2022/06/28/americans-complex-views-on-gender-identity-and -transgender-issues. Accessed October 18, 2022.

14. Jonathan Morrow and David Kinnaman, *Gen Z: The Culture, Beliefs and Motivations Shaping the Next Generation* (Barna Group in connection with Impact 360 Institute, 2018), 46.

15. Jeffrey M. Jones, "LGBT Identification Rises to 5.6% in Latest U.S. Estimate," Gallup, February 24, 2021, https://news.gallup.com/poll /329708/lgbt-identification-rises-latest-estimate.aspx.

16. Antoinette Bueno, "Miley Cyrus Met Her amfAR Agender Date Tyler Ford Through Ariana Grande," *Entertainment Tonight*, June 17, 2015, https:// www.etonline.com/news/166362_miley_cyrus_met_her_amfar_agender _date_tyler_ford_through_ariana_grande.

17. Serena Sonoma, "New Study Reveals Zoomers Are More Likely to Think Outside the Gender and Sexuality Box," *Them*, July 2, 2020, https:// www.them.us/story/zoomers-more-likely-to-think-outside-the-gender -and-sexuality-box.

18. Sara Ashley O'Brien, "Tinder Adds Sexual Orientation Feature to Aid LGBTQ Matching," *CNN Business*, June 4, 2019, https://www.cnn.com /2019/06/04/tech/tinder-glaad-sexual-orientation. Accessed April 8, 2021.

19. Kim Parker and Ruth Igielnik, "On the Cusp of Adulthood and Facing an Uncertain Future: What We Know about Gen Z So Far" (Pew

Research Center, May 14, 2020), https://www.pewresearch.org/social
-trends/2020/05/14/on-the-cusp-of-adulthood-and-facing-an-uncertain
-future-what-we-know-about-gen-z-so-far-2. Accessed February 9, 2021.

20. Jason Jimenez, *Challenging Conversations: A Practical Guide to Discuss Controversial Topics in the Church* (Grand Rapids, MI: Baker Publishing Group, 2020), 184.

21. Anne Loehr, "Generation Z: Conservative or Liberal?," *Medium*, August 25, 2017, https://medium.com/@anneloehr/generation-z-conservative-or -liberal-8a77373e2c6e. Accessed May 20, 2023.

22. Jean M. Twenge, *iGen: Why Today's Super-Connected Kids Are Growing Up Less Rebellious, More Tolerant, Less Happy—and Completely Unprepared for Adulthood—and What That Means for the Rest of Us* (New York: Atria Paperbacks, Kindle Edition, 2017), 278.

23. Morrow and Kinnaman, *Gen Z*, 58.

24. Anna Wilkinson, "Opinion: Gen Z Is Too Sensitive," *Scot Scoop News*, January 11, 2021, https://scotscoop.com/gen-z-is-too-sensitive. Accessed September 8, 2022.

25. "Free Expression on College Campuses," Knight Foundation, May 13, 2019, https://knightfoundation.org/reports/free-expression-college -campuses. Accessed May 20, 2023.

26. Greg Lukianoff and Jonathan Haidt, *The Coddling of the American Mind: How Good Intentions and Bad Ideas Are Setting Up a Generation for Failure* (New York: Penguin Books, 2018), 6.

27. "Microaggression," https://www.merriam-webster.com/dictionary /microaggression.

28. Alan Levinovitz, "How Trigger Warnings Silence Religious Students," *The Atlantic*, Aug. 30, 2016, https://www.theatlantic.com/politics /archive/2016/08/silencing-religious-students-on-campus/497951. Accessed March 2021.

29. Lukianoff and Haidt, *Coddling*, 41–42.

30. Although most of Gen Z embrace diversity, there is, however, a lot of confusion over how to refer to someone of a different color. To avoid coming off as racially insensitive, students will even avoid asking another student where they are from. Bradley Campbell and Jason Manning wrote a book called *The Rise of Victimhood Culture: Microaggressions, Safe Spaces, and the New Culture Wars* (Palgrave Macmillan, 2018) in an attempt to reduce the political correctness that is being forced on a young generation besieged by victimization.

31. Renee Stepler, "Led by Baby Boomers, Divorce Rates Climb for America's 50+ Population" (Pew Research Center, March 9, 2017), https://www .pewresearch.org/fact-tank/2017/03/09/led-by-baby-boomers-divorce-rates -climb-for-americas-50-population. Accessed October 18, 2022.

CHAPTER TWO: A LOOK AT THE PARENTS RAISING GEN Z

1. Angela Woo, "The Forgotten Generation: Let's Talk about Generation X," *Forbes*, November 14, 2018, https://www.forbes.com/sites /forbesagencycouncil/2018/11/14/the-forgotten-generation-lets-talk -about-generation-x. Accessed March 18, 2021.
2. If you are a Gen X parent, I recommend my parenting book written with Alex McFarland, *Abandoned Faith: Why Millennials Are Walking Away and How You Can Lead Them Home* (Colorado Springs, CO: Focus on the Family, 2017).
3. Susan Gregory Thomas, "A Teacher's Guide to Generation X Parents," *Edutopia*, George Lucas Educational Foundation, January 19, 2010, https://www.edutopia.org/generation-x-parents-relationships-guide. Accessed March 8, 2021.
4. "Millennial Parents: 6 Surprising Ways They're Raising Kids Differently," quoting research from Boston College's Center for Work and Family, *KinderCare Learning* (blog), 2016, https://www.kindercare.com/content -hub/articles/2016/may/millennial-moms-dads-6-ways-theyre-raising-kids -differently.
5. Sharon Greenthal, "How Millennial Parents Are Raising Their Children Differently," Verywell Family, November 24, 2020, https://www .verywellfamily.com/millennial-parents-raising-children-4158549 #citation-3, quoting from The United States Census Bureau, "The Majority of Children Live with Two Parents," November 17, 2016, https://www.census.gov/newsroom/press-releases/2016/cb16-192.html.
6. Gary J. Gates, "Marriage and Family: LGBT Individuals and Same-Sex Couples," *The Future of Children*, vol. 25, no. 2 (Princeton University, 2015), 72, https://www.jstor.org/stable/43581973.
7. Jerry McCall, "5 Things Millennial Parents Are Doing Better Than Their Parents," FamilyLife, 2019, https://www.familylife.com/articles/topics /parenting/ages-and-stages/young-children/5-things-millennial-parents -are-doing-better-than-their-parents. Accessed January 13, 2021.

CHAPTER THREE: THREE PARENTING FLAWS AFFECTING GEN Z

1. Gary R. Collins, *Christian Counseling: A Comprehensive Guide*, 3rd ed. (Wheaton, IL: Nelson Reference and Electronic, 2007), 142–43.

CHAPTER FOUR: DIGITAL OBSESSION AND ITS DANGEROUS EFFECTS

1. Sean McDowell and J. Warner Wallace, *So the Next Generation Will Know: Preparing Young Christians for a Challenging World* (Colorado Springs, CO: David C Cook, Kindle Edition, 2019), 52–53.
2. Benita Matofska and Sophie Sheinwald, *Generation Share: The Change-Makers Building the Sharing Economy* (Bristol, UK: Policy Press, 2019), 57.
3. Victoria Rideout, Alanna Peebles, Supreet Mann, and Michael Robb,

The Common Sense Census: Media Use by Tweens and Teens, 2021 (San Francisco: Common Sense, 2022), 3, 5, https://www.commonsensemedia.org/research/the-common-sense-census-media-use-by-tweens-and-teens-2021.

4. "Meet Generation Z: Forget Everything You Learned about Millennials," Sparks and Honey, June 17, 2014, http://www.slideshare.net/sparksandhoney/generation-z-final-june-17.

5. Tim Elmore, *Artificial Maturity: Helping Kids Meet the Challenge of Becoming Authentic Adults* (San Francisco: Jossey-Bass, 2012), 4.

6. Tim Elmore and Andrew McPeak, *Generation Z Unfiltered: Facing Nine Hidden Challenges of the Most Anxious Population* (Atlanta, Poet Gardner, Kindle Edition, 2019), 202.

7. "Half of Gen Z Feel Bad about the Amount of Time Spent on Screens" (Barna Group, February 10, 2021), https://www.barna.com/research/gen-z-screens. Accessed May 20, 2023.

8. Laura Hancock, ed., *Gen Z: Rethinking Culture* (Halesowen, UK: Youth for Christ, 2016), 11, https://yfc.co.uk/rethinkingculture. Accessed January 2021.

9. Matt Walsh, *Church of Cowards: A Wake-Up Call to Complacent Christians* (Washington, DC: Regnery Gateway, Kindle Edition, 2020), 130.

10. Elmore and McPeak, *Generation Z Unfiltered*, 56–57.

11. AAP Council on Communications and Media, "Media Use in School-Aged Children and Adolescents," *Pediatrics* 138, no. 5 (November 2016), https://doi.org/10.1542/peds.2016-2592.

12. Dr. Nicole Beurkens, "Is Screen Time Affecting Your Kid's Memory?," Qustodio, September 20, 2022, https://www.qustodio.com/en/blog/screen-time-memory. Accessed October 18, 2022.

13. Jean M. Twenge, *iGen: Why Today's Super-Connected Kids Are Growing Up Less Rebellious, More Tolerant, Less Happy—and Completely Unprepared for Adulthood* (New York: Atria Paperbacks, Kindle Edition, 2017), 97.

14. The Data Team, "Generation Z Is Stressed, Depressed and Exam-Obsessed," *The Economist*, February 27, 2019, https://www.economist.com/graphic-detail/2019/02/27/generation-z-is-stressed-depressed-and-exam-obsessed.

15. Kashmira Gander, "Gen Z Is the Most Stressed Out Group in America, Poll Finds," *Newsweek*, October 20, 2020, https://www.newsweek.com/gen-z-most-stressed-out-group-america-poll-finds-1540549.

16. Kristinova V. Justimbaste, "Teen Depression Linked to Excessive Screen Time, Study Shows," *The Christian Post*, November 16, 2017, https://www.christianpost.com/trends/teen-depression-linked-to-excessive-screen-time-study-shows.html.

17. *Gen Z: Vol. 2: Caring for Young Souls and Cultivating Resilience* (Barna Group in connection with Impact 360 Institute, 2020), 22.

18. Sean Mahoney, ed., *Gen Z 2025: The Final Generation* (Sparks and Honey,

LLC, 2015), 56, https://www.sparksandhoney.com/reports-list/2018/10/5/generation-z-2025-the-final-generation.

19. National Sleep Foundation, "Sleepy Connected Americans," ScienceDaily, March 11, 2011, www.sciencedaily.com/releases/2011/03/110307065350.htm.

20. Lakshmi, "Everything Parents Should Know about Children Watching Porn," Mobicip, October 6, 2020, https://www.mobicip.com/blog/everything-parents-should-know-about-children-watching-porn. Accessed October 18, 2022.

21. "Data and Statistics about ADHD," Centers for Disease Control and Prevention, August 9, 2022, https://www.cdc.gov/ncbddd/adhd/data.html. Accessed October 18, 2022.

22. The Data Team, "Generation Z Is Stressed."

23. "Rising Parental Expectations Linked to Perfectionism in College Students," American Psychological Association, March 31, 2022, https://www.apa.org/news/press/releases/2022/03/parental-expectations-perfectionism. Accessed October 19, 2022.

24. Nick Morrison, "Students Turn to Study Drugs and Alcohol to Cope with Campus Life," *Forbes*, February 13, 2019, https://www.forbes.com/sites/nickmorrison/2019/02/13/students-turn-to-study-drugs-and-alcohol-to-cope-with-campus-life. Accessed October 19, 2022.

25. Jonathan McKee, *Parenting Generation Screen: Guiding Your Kids to Be Wise in a Digital World* (Colorado Springs, CO: Focus on the Family, Kindle Edition, 2021), 6.

26. "National Study: Teen Misuse and Abuse of Prescription Drugs Up 33 Percent Since 2008, Stimulants Contributing to Sustained Rx Epidemic," Partnership to End Addiction, April 23, 2013, https://drugfree.org/newsroom/news-item/national-study-teen-misuse-and-abuse-of-prescription-drugs-up-33-percent-since-2008-stimulants-contributing-to-sustained-rx-epidemic. Accessed September 8, 2022.

27. Deborah Tannen, *You Just Don't Understand: Women and Men in Conversation* (New York: William Morrow Paperbacks, 2007), 23–48.

CHAPTER FIVE: DEPLETED FAITH

1. Ryan P. Burge, "Gen Z and Religion in 2021," *Religion in Public* (blog), June 15, 2022, https://religioninpublic.blog/2022/06/15/gen-z-and-religion-in-2021. Accessed October 18, 2022.

2. Jonathan Morrow and David Kinnaman, *Gen Z: The Culture, Beliefs and Motivations Shaping the Next Generation* (Barna Group in connection with Impact 360 Institute, 2018), 62–63.

3. Paul David Tripp, *Age of Opportunity: A Biblical Guide to Parenting Teens* (Phillipsburg, NJ: P & R Publishing, 2001), 16.

4. Morrow and Kinnaman, *Gen Z*, 25–26.

5. "Atheism Doubles Among Generation Z" (Barna Group, January 24, 2018), https://www.barna.com/research/atheism-doubles-among-generation-z. Accessed March 17, 2021.

6. James Emery White, *Meet Generation Z: Understanding and Reaching the New Post-Christian World* (Grand Rapids, MI: Baker Books, Kindle version, 2017), 62.

7. Dietrich Bonhoeffer, *The Cost of Discipleship* (New York: Macmillan Publishing, 1963), 47–48.

8. Bonhoeffer, *Cost of Discipleship*, 47–48.

9. You can subscribe to my YouTube channel (search for "Jason P. Jimenez") for biblical worldview content. Another helpful YouTube channel is "What Would You Say?" by The Colson Center.

10. Morrow and Kinnaman, *Gen Z*, 78.

11. Morrow and Kinnaman, *Gen Z*, 62.

12. Resources to help you defend God's existence: Norman L. Geisler and Frank Turek, *I Don't Have Enough Faith to Be an Atheist* (Wheaton, IL: Crossway Books, 2004); Jason Jimenez and Alex McFarland, *Stand Strong in Your Faith: Live What You Believe with Confidence and Passion* (Racine, WI: BroadStreet Publishing Group, 2017); Richard E. Simmons III, *Reflections on the Existence of God: A Series of Essays* (Birmingham, AL: Union Hill Publishing, 2019). Many more free resources are available at bethinking.org/does-god-exist.

13. Norman L. Geisler and Jason Jimenez, *The Bible's Answers to 100 of Life's Biggest Questions* (Grand Rapids, MI: Baker Books, 2015), 53–55.

CHAPTER SIX: CHALLENGING CONVERSATIONS TO HAVE WITH YOUR KIDS ABOUT SEX, GENDER IDENTITY, AND PORN

1. Phil Keren, "Mayor Calls for Ohio School Board to Resign over Material Suggesting Kids Write about Sex, Drinking," *USA Today*, Gannett Satellite Information Network, September 15, 2021, https://www.usatoday.com/story/news/nation/2021/09/15/hudson-mayor-school-board-must-resign-after-students-write-sex-alcohol/8346222002. Accessed November 19, 2021.

2. Jessica Chasmar, "Texas Mom Erupts at School Board over 'Anal Sex' Passage in Middle Schoolers' Book, *FOX News Network*, September 21, 2021, https://www.foxnews.com/us/texas-mom-school-board-anal-sex-book. Accessed October 8, 2021.

3. Dana Kennedy, "Dalton Parents Enraged over 'Masturbation' Videos for First-Graders," *New York Post*, May 29, 2021, https://nypost.com/2021/05/29/dalton-parents-enraged-over-masturbation-videos-for-1st-graders. Accessed June 2, 2021.

4. Tim Challies, "God Hates Sexual Immorality," *Challies* (blog), December 24, 2016, https://www.challies.com/articles/god-hates-sexual-immorality.

5. Jason Jimenez, *Challenging Conversations: A Practical Guide to Discuss Controversial Topics in the Church* (Grand Rapids, MI: Baker Books, 2020), 82.
6. Take advantage of the resources provided by Focus on the Family at focusonthefamily.com/tag/pornography.

CHAPTER SEVEN: CHALLENGING CONVERSATIONS TO HAVE WITH YOUR KIDS ABOUT DEPRESSION, SUICIDE, ABORTION, AND RACISM

1. "Mental Health Disorder Statistics," Johns Hopkins Medicine, https://www.hopkinsmedicine.org/health/wellness-and-prevention/mental-health-disorder-statistics. Accessed October 19, 2022.
2. Mitch Aldridge, "Only 29% of Gen Z Believe Abortion Is Morally Wrong," *Impact 360 Institute* (blog), quoting *Gen Z: Vol. 2 Launch* (Impact 360 Institute in connection with Barna Group, 2020), https://www.impact360institute.org/articles/only-29-of-gen-z-believe-abortion-is-morally-wrong.
3. See John Ensor and Scott Klusendorf's book *Stand for Life: A Student's Guide for Making the Case and Saving Lives* (Peabody, MA: Hendrickson Publishers, 2012).
4. Francis J. Beckwith, *Politically Correct Death: Answering the Arguments for Abortion Rights* (Grand Rapids, MI: Baker Publishing Group, 1993), 112.
5. Russell Moore and Andrew T. Walker, eds., *The Gospel and Racial Reconciliation*, in The Gospel for Life series (Nashville: B&H, 2016), 3.
6. "Genetics vs. Genomics Fact Sheet," National Human Genome Research Institute, September 7, 2018, https://www.genome.gov/about-genomics/fact-sheets/Genetics-vs-Genomics. Accessed October 19, 2022.

CHAPTER EIGHT: BUILD YOUR HOUSE ON *LOVE*

1. Ron Deal, "Living in a Stepfamily," Focus on the Family, 2007, https://www.focusonthefamily.com/parenting/living-in-a-stepfamily. Accessed March 19, 2021.
2. Tom Junod, "My Friend Mister Rogers," *The Atlantic*, December 2019, https://www.theatlantic.com/magazine/archive/2019/12/what-would-mister-rogers-do/600772. Accessed September 19, 2022.
3. Inga Kiderra, "Lied-to Children More Likely to Cheat and Lie," *UC San Diego Today*, March 18, 2014, https://today.ucsd.edu/story/lied_to_children_more_likely_to_cheat_and_lie.

CHAPTER NINE: DISCIPLINE IN THE HOME

1. Tedd Tripp, *Shepherding a Child's Heart* (Wapwallopen, PA: Shepherd Press, 1995), xviii.
2. Danny Huerta, "Is Spanking Biblical?," Focus on the Family, 2018,

https://www.focusonthefamily.com/parenting/is-spanking-biblical. Accessed June 1, 2021.

3. There is a sizeable percentage of Gen Zers who seek to listen to various perspectives and appreciate diverse voices on a range of topics, but Gen Z is in desperate need of their parents, the church, and reasonable voices in the social media world to teach them how to engage while respecting the complexity of other people's opinions—whether or not they agree.

4. Dr. Scott Turansky and Joanne Miller, *The Christian Parenting Handbook: 50 Heart-Based Strategies for All the Stages of Your Child's Life* (Nashville: Thomas Nelson, 2013), 11.

5. Turansky and Miller, *Christian Parenting Handbook*, 11.

6. Daniel P. Huerta, *7 Traits of Effective Parenting* (Colorado Springs, CO: Focus on the Family, 2020).

CHAPTER TEN: THREE ADJUSTMENTS YOU (ALMOST CERTAINLY) NEED TO MAKE

1. I recommend you read Justin Whitmel Earley's *The Common Rule: Habits of Purpose for an Age of Distraction* (Downers Grove, IL: InterVarsity Press, 2019).

2. Michael Zigarelli, "Distracted from God: A Five-Year, Worldwide Study," Christianity 9 to 5, 2008, http://www.christianity9to5.org/distracted-from -god. Accessed June 15, 2021.

3. John Mark Comer, *The Ruthless Elimination of Hurry: How to Stay Emotionally Healthy and Spiritually Alive in the Chaos of the Modern World* (Colorado Springs, CO: Waterbrook, 2019), 22, 27.

4. Lisa Van De Gyen, "Are You Signing Up Your Kids for Too Many Activities?," ParentsCanada, October 10, 2019, https://www.parentscanada.com/school /are-you-signing-up-your-kids-for-too-many-activities. Accessed August 3, 2021.

5. Patrick A. Coleman, "6 Scientific Reasons Family Dinners Are Important for Your Child," Fatherly, February 8, 2017, https://www.fatherly.com/health -science/6-reasons-eating-family-dinner. Accessed November 12, 2021.

CHAPTER ELEVEN: MODEL YOUR FAITH AT HOME AND BEYOND

1. Paul E. Miller, *A Praying Life: Connecting with God in a Distracting World* (Colorado Springs, CO: NavPress, 2017), 8.

2. Sean McDowell and J. Warner Wallace, *So the Next Generation Will Know: Preparing Young Christians for a Challenging World* (Colorado Springs, CO: David C Cook, Kindle Edition, 2019), 89.

3. Ryan P. Burge, "The Possible Decline of the Nones Isn't a Boost for Evangelicals," *Christianity Today*, March 3, 2020, https://www .christianitytoday.com/news/2020/march/nones-decline-generation-z -millennial-faith-research.html.

4. If a person has a distorted view of love, then everything else will be out of sorts. Life isn't about selfishness. It's about demonstrating the sacrificial love of Christ to others. The Bible says, "Each of you should use whatever gift you have received to serve others, as faithful stewards of God's grace in its various forms" (1 Peter 4:10, NIV). However, when you live to serve yourself, you miss out on opportunities for God to use you. Volunteering and helping others are vibrant ways to live a life of significance and to impact the world.

CHAPTER TWELVE: FIVE WAYS TO FEED THEIR FUTURES
1. Shaunti Feldhahn and Lisa A. Rice, *For Parents Only: Getting Inside the Head of Your Kid* (Colorado Springs, CO: Multnomah Books, 2007), 43.
2. Amy Morin, "7 Scientifically Proven Benefits of Gratitude," *Psychology Today*, April 3, 2015, https://www.psychologytoday.com/us/blog/what -mentally-strong-people-dont-do/201504/7-scientifically-proven-benefits -gratitude.
3. Bill Burnett and Dave Evans, *Designing Your Life: How to Build a Well-Lived, Joyful Life* (New York: Alfred A. Knopf, 2016), 5.
4. Matt Mullenweg, "In Memoriam: Chuck Mullenweg," *Unlucky in Cards* (blog), April 20, 2016, https://ma.tt/2016/04/in-memoriam-chuck -mullenweg. Accessed November 14, 2021.
5. Marilyn Price-Mitchell, "Goal-Setting Is Linked to Higher Achievement," *Psychology Today*, March 14, 2018, https://www.psychologytoday.com/us /blog/the-moment-youth/201803/goal-setting-is-linked-higher-achievement. Accessed October 21, 2022.
6. Greg Lukianoff and Jonathan Haidt, *The Coddling of the American Mind: How Good Intentions and Bad Ideas Are Setting Up a Generation for Failure* (New York: Penguin Books, 2018), 185.

CHAPTER THIRTEEN: SANITY FOR SINGLE PARENTS
1. Dallas Willard, *Life without Lack: Living in the Fullness of Psalm 23* (Nashville: Nelson Books, Kindle Edition, 2018), 202–203.
2. "Resilience," https://www.dictionary.com/browse/resilience.
3. Kathy Koch, *Resilient Kids: Raising Them to Embrace Life with Confidence* (Chicago: Moody Publishers, 2022).

CONCLUSION: FEELING STUCK IN A NEVER-ENDING MAZE?
1. Caleb Kaltenbach, *Messy Truth: How to Foster Community without Sacrificing Conviction* (Colorado Springs, CO: WaterBrook, 2021), 17.
2. Oswald Chambers, *My Utmost for His Highest*, "The Big Compelling of God" (online devotional), https://utmost.org/classic/the-big-compelling-of -god-classic. Accessed September 22, 2022.

FOCUS ON THE FAMILY®

LAUNCH™
INTO THE
◄ TEEN YEARS ►

RELATIONSHIPS. PUBERTY. "THE TALK."

Not sure how to discuss these with your preteen? We've got you. Tackle topics like identity, dating, and more with *Launch Into the Teen Years*.

The video-based lessons will give you and your preteen a biblical foundation for adolescence. *Launch Into the Teen Years* comes with a parent guide, a journal for your child, questions, activities, and helpful tips. Your preteen will learn about these topics from someone – make sure they learn the truth from you!

LaunchIntoTheTeenYears.com

CP1939